INVESTIGATING HISTORY

A WORLD STUDY AFTER 1900

FOUNDATION EDITION

John D. Clare

Hodder Murray
www.hoddereducation.co.uk

Acknowledgements

The publishers would like to thank the following individuals, institutions and companies for permission to reproduce copyright illustrations in this book:

A & M University: p4; Imperial War Museum: p6, p8, p41, p61 (top); Wellcome Library, London: p11; Mary Evans: p17 (The Woman's Library); p18; p19 (Fawcett Library), p39 (Alexander Meledin), p47, p48; Hulton-Deutsch: p22, Topham Picturepoint: p26, p34; Bildarchiv Preußischer Kulturbesitz: p25; AKG London: p30; David Low, Evening Standard, and for supply of photo Centre for the Study of Cartoons and Caricature, University of Kent, Canterbury, CT2 7NU: p32; David King Collection: p39, p45; Peter Newark's American Pictures: p51; Corbis/Seattle Post-Intelligencer Collection; Museum of History & Industry: p53; Advertising Archives: p54; Hulton Archive: p60; Topham AP: p61 (bottom); The Wiener Library: p64; Institute of Contemporary History and Wiener Library limited/David Olere: p67, p72; Zofja Rozenstrauch; Rubin Mass Ltd., Jerusalem: p69; Bettman/Corbis: p79, p81; Corbis: p80; Ranan Lurie N.Y: p.82; Kevin Weaver/ Hulton Archive: p86, p89; Associated Press: p88; Popperfoto/Reuters: p91.

The publishers would also like to thank the following for permission to reproduce material in this book:
Simon & Schuster UK for extracts from The End of the American Century by Jeffery Robinson Copyright © Jeffery Robinson, 1997; University Press of the Pacific for extracts from Through the Russian Revolution by Albert Rhys Williams; Pen and Sword Books Ltd for extracts from Veterans by Richard van Emden and Steve Humphries; The Estate of Florence Farmborough c/o Constable & Robinson Ltd for extracts from A Nurse at the Russian Front 1914–18 by Florence Farmborough, 1974; Penguin for extracts from This Way for the Gas, Ladies and Gentlemen by Tadeusz Borowski © Penguin Book Ltd, 1967, and extracts from Total War by Peter Calvocoressi and Guy Wint, 1972, © Peter Calvocoressi and Guy Wint 1972; The Orion Publishing group for extracts from My American Century by Studs Terkel published by Pheonix Press and extracts from Keep Smiling Through the Home Front by Susan Briggs published by Weidenfeld & Nicolson; Oxford University Press for extracts from The Oxford Companion to the Second World War by A N Frankland; HarperCollins Publishers for extracts from A History of the Soviet Union by Geoffrey Hosking, © 1985 Geoffrey Hosking; Sheil Land Associates for extracts from Night by Elie Wiesel, published by Penguin Copyright © Les Editions de Minuit, 1958; The Random House Group for extracts from My War gone by, I miss it so by Anthony Loyd published by Doubleday. Used by permission of Transworld Publishers, a division of The Random House Group Limited.

Every effort has been made to trace and acknowledge ownership of copyright. The publishers will be glad to make suitable arrangements with any copyright holders whom it has not been possible to contact.

Artwork by Chris Rothero from Beehive Illustration and Richard Morris.

Orders: please contact Bookpoint Ltd, 130 Milton Park, Abingdon, Oxon OX14 4SB. Telephone: (44) 01235 827720. Fax: (44) 01235 400454. Lines are open from 9.00 - 6.00, Monday to Saturday, with a 24 hour message answering service. You can also order through our website www.hoddereducation.co.uk.

British Library Cataloguing in Publication Data
A catalogue record for this title is available from the British Library

ISBN-10: 0 340 86912 7
ISBN-13: 978 0 340 86912 3

First Published 2003
Impression number   10 9 8 7 6 5 4 3
Year   2007 2006 2005

Copyright © 2003 John D. Clare

Cover photo from a painting by Coline U. Gill, 'Heavy Artillery' © Imperial War Museum
Layout by Cathy May (Endangered Species).
Colour Reproduction by Dot Gradations Ltd, UK
Printed in Dubai for Hodder Murray, a division of Hodder Headline, 338 Euston Road, London NW1 3BH.

CONTENTS

INTRODUCTION
The Twentieth Century – an Overview

History and the broken supermarket trolley

In 1900, people were looking forward to the next 100 years.   They thought the world was going to get better and better.   They thought that machines would make everyone rich, and every job easy.   They hoped that **democracy** would make the world a better place for everyone. 5

But history – like a broken supermarket trolley – had a mind of its own!   Things did not turn out how people hoped. 10

SOURCE A

Even at the start of the century, the countries of Europe were getting ready for war.   They wanted more and more land.   They were building up their armies.   They joined 15 together against other countries – Britain joined with France and Russia, Germany joined with Austria.   The two sides hated each other. 20

Today, Science is very clever … and frightening! This is CC, the world's first cloned kitten.   Some scientists say they have cloned human beings. Should we let them do this?

Impact of World Wars

In 1914, the two sides went to war. That war became the first world war – people called it the ²⁵ 'Great War' because so many countries joined the fighting. Everyone was happy to go to war – millions of men 'joined up'.

The Great War (1914–1918) ³⁰ changed people's ideas. More than eight million soldiers died in the First World War. Ever since, many people have said that war is a bad thing.

³⁵ In some countries, people decided that democracy was a bad thing too. A **Communist** government took over Russia in 1917. **Fascist**

governments came to power in Italy (1922) and Germany (1933) – they ⁴⁰ were evil, **racist** governments. Both Italy and Germany started to take land from other countries by force. In the far east, Japan's ruler joined with Germany and Italy and ⁴⁵ started to conquer other countries.

In 1939 a Second World War (1939–1945) broke out.

The Second World War led to the defeat of fascism, but soon another ⁵⁰ war broke out – the '**Cold War**' between America and Russia. Everyone was frightened that the atom bomb would kill us all.

The New Terror ⁵⁵

In 1900, the countries of Europe 'owned' empires with land all over the world. After 1945, many countries got **independence**.

But many of these new countries ⁶⁰ are still very poor, and there have been **revolutions** and wars in many parts of the world.

Also, today, people are very frightened of **terrorism**. This ⁶⁵ book ends with the terrorist attacks on America on 11 September 2001. It is thought that these attacks were carried out by Muslim terrorists. ⁷⁰

THINK ABOUT IT

1. 'Always look on the bright side of life' – why were people hopeful in 1900?

2. Why were the years after 1918 bad for democracy?

3. What were the good, and the bad, results of the Second World War?

4. Can we look forward to the 21st century? Think about:
   - wars and terrorism,
   - science,
   - hunger and world poverty.

   Divide into two sides and debate what you think as a class.

CHAPTER 1

War and Change
How did the First World War change British society?

In this chapter you will:

- Learn why men went to fight in the First World War.
- Learn why some men's ideas about war changed.
- Find out what it was like to fight in the war.
- Think about how the war changed the lives of British women.

SOURCE Ⓐ *British soldiers off to war.   Can you see the wire-cutters on their guns? This was to cut through the German barbed wire in an attack – but most of these soldiers were shot before they got near the German barbed wire.*

When the First World War – the 'Great War' as people called it then – broke out in 1914, British men were VERY happy to go to

5 fight. In the first two months, 736,000 men joined up. Everyone thought the war would be over by Christmas, and joining up was a good way to look brave in front of

10 the girls.

THINK ABOUT IT

1. Read Source B. Make a list of all the reasons why Robert Burns joined the army in 1914.
Which do you think was more important for him – patriotism (fighting for his country) or adventure and fun?

2. Sometimes men who did not join up were insulted and attacked.
Can you think why?

3. Do you think young people are as patriotic today as they were in 1914? Give reasons for your opinion.

4. Source B is a recount text.
Re-write the source as a formal report, explaining why this man joined up in 1914. Make sure you:
- use formal language,
- use the third person ('he'), not the first person ('I'),
- take a paragraph for each reason he joined up.

SOURCE B

In 1914, Robert Burns's parents had a hotel in Scotland. He said this about why he went to join up in 1914:

Everywhere you went in Glasgow there were great big pictures pointing at you, saying: 'Your King And Country Need You'. They seemed to be pointing just at *you*.

I thought to myself, I am going to do something about this, so I went to join up. They asked me how old I was. I said I was 18, and they said: 'Oh, you are too young – go back home to your mother'.

When I told my friend what had happened, he told me to tell a little fib. You had to be 19 to join up in those days, so I said I was 19 – it was only a little fib, because I was only two months off being 19. So I told my fib, and I was in the army.

I think I joined up because I thought it would be fun. I was too young to understand about **patriotism**. I lived in the country, and I thought it would be like going on a picnic to a far-away place with some friends. We all thought the war would be over by Christmas. When I told my boss he said: 'Well, it will be a nice 6-month holiday for you – yes, join up'.

At 18 and 19 years old, you are not very clever.

Everybody else was joining up, so I thought, if they are doing it, why can't I? Also, my father had joined up right at the start of the war, and I wanted to copy him.

By the end of the war ALL my family had joined up, and my mother was left to run the hotel on her own.

Robert Burns was remembering this in 1997, when he was 103 years old.

How did the government persuade men to enlist?

Conscription is where a government tells men they HAVE to join up. The
5 British government did not use conscription until 1916.

Volunteers are men
10 who go to join up because they want to fight. In 1914, ALL the British soldiers were volunteers.

15 To encourage British men to volunteer, the government had to use **propaganda** – ways to change
20 people's thinking so that they hated the evil 'Huns' (Germans) and wanted to go to kill them.

SOURCE Ⓐ

The Red Cross helped soldiers on both sides.

The Iron Cross is a German medal.

The artist makes the Germans look evil and nasty.

RED CROSS OR IRON CROSS?

WOUNDED AND A PRISONER OUR SOLDIER CRIES FOR WATER.
THE GERMAN "SISTER" POURS IT ON THE GROUND BEFORE HIS EYES.
THERE IS NO WOMAN IN BRITAIN WHO WOULD DO IT.
THERE IS NO WOMAN IN BRITAIN WHO WILL FORGET IT.

A wounded British soldier asks a German nurse for water.

This British poster tried to make people hate the Germans. It shows German nurses looking after wounded British prisoners of war.

White Feather campaign

25   The government tried to make men who did not volunteer feel bad.   It said they were cowards. It said they did not care about their
30 country.   It said they were letting down their families.   Women gave white feathers to men who did not volunteer – to show they were cowards.

35 The government also said that men who joined together could fight together.   So men could join up with their friends.   These units were called 'Pals' units.   Men from
40 the same town could all be in the same unit.   A football team could join up and stay together.   This worked well, and many men joined up with their pals.

45 Some men joined up because the army paid better wages than the job they were doing.

  Some criminals were given the choice of joining up instead of
50 going to prison.

  Some men said it was wrong to fight.   They were called **'Conscientious Objectors'** ('COs') because their conscience (beliefs)
55 made them object to (hate) war. There were 16,500 COs in the first World War.

Conscientious Objectors

COs still had to go to war.   The government let them go as nurses   60 and ambulance drivers – saving lives not taking them.

If the COs refused even to do this, they were put in prison. If a man refused to fight on the   65 battlefield, he was shot.

THINK ABOUT IT

Look at Source A.   Explain why it was very good at getting men to join up. Use these ideas to help you:
- The way it portrays the German soldiers and the German nurse.
- The difference between 'Red Cross' and 'Iron Cross'.
- What men seeing the poster would have felt.

STOP AND REFLECT: Why did men go to fight in the First World War? Write a paragraph starting: 'Men went to fight in the First World War because ...'

Why did some soldiers' views about the war change?

The reality

Lots of men, like Robert Burns, joined up because they thought it would be a bit of fun. When they
5 got there, they found that war is not fun. Many soldiers came to hate the war.

Many men hated the war, but they could not run away. They did not want to be called a coward. 10

Many men wanted to be wounded – not badly, but just badly enough to have to go home.

A bullet in the arm or the leg was what they wanted. They called 15 this 'a **Blighty** one' ('Blighty' was the name they had for Britain). If your friend got 'a Blighty one' in a battle, you were very happy for him. 20

However, soldiers did NOT like men who shot themselves, or who tried to get a Blighty one (see Source A). They said they were cowards. They believed that 25 soldiers should stick together and not let the other men down.

SOURCE A

This is a story that Robert Burns told about the Battle of Loos (1915).

It was terrible in the war, but you learned to put up with it. You got used to it, but you wanted it all to end. Everyone wanted a Blighty one – a wound in the arm or the hand that would get you back home. I hoped to get a Blighty one, but it was difficult to get one in the right place.

At the Battle of Loos, the chap next to me had his legs in the air.

I said: 'Keep your legs down. You'll get shot.'

He said: 'I want to get shot in the leg. I want a Blighty one so I can go home. I don't want to get shot in the body.'

Then another man said: 'Good idea', and he did the same.

Remembered by Robert Burns in 1998.

THINK ABOUT IT

1. Does Source A prove that all the British soldiers hated the war?

2. Do you think that soldiers who got themselves shot on purpose were cowards?

3. Men who wounded themselves on purpose were sent to the firing squad. Was the army right to do this?

4. Look at Sources A and B again carefully.

   Write about the way men's views about war changed when they got to the Front and started fighting.

Use these sentence starters to help you:

- At the start of the war, soldiers like Robert Burns wanted to go and fight because …

- However, when they started fighting, they found …

- Many men – even Robert Burns – hoped that …

- Some men wanted to go home so badly that they …

- So, it seems that men's views about the war changed …

SOURCE B

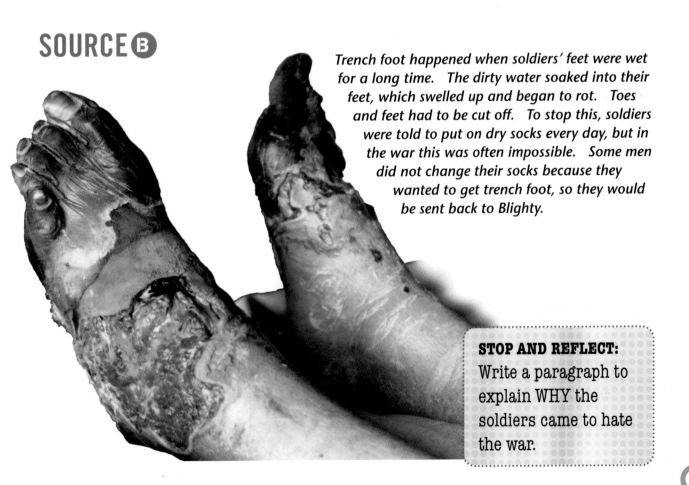

Trench foot happened when soldiers' feet were wet for a long time. The dirty water soaked into their feet, which swelled up and began to rot. Toes and feet had to be cut off. To stop this, soldiers were told to put on dry socks every day, but in the war this was often impossible. Some men did not change their socks because they wanted to get trench foot, so they would be sent back to Blighty.

STOP AND REFLECT:
Write a paragraph to explain WHY the soldiers came to hate the war.

What was life like in the trenches?

For most of the First World War, the men fought from trenches (see page 14).

5 There were times when the Germans shelled the trenches, or when the soldiers had to go on an

10 attack. During these times, they would be very frightened.

But, for much of the time, life was boring.

15 Even at the front, they spent most of the day doing boring jobs like digging and look-out duty. And

20 soldiers only spent about 4–8 days in the front line. After that, they would go for a few days in the

25 support trenches, and then they would be given a few days away from the front, where they could

30 wash and get 'deloused' (get rid of the small insects called **lice**).

SOURCE Ⓐ

▶January 1915◀

TRENCH NEWS

Beginner's Special

THE ARMY'S GOOD FOOD GUIDE

Do you like animals? Are you fond of dogs? Then trench sausages are just the thing for you! And if you have the runs, then our specially trained chefs have the cure ...

GET TO KNOW YOUR WAY AROUND THE TRENCH SYSTEM:

ADVERTISEMENT:

New stock of lice just in!

HOW TO SURVIVE – DO'S AND DON'T'S

HOW TO AVOID TRENCH FOOT:

HOW TO GET RID OF LICE:

What happens to your feet if you get trench foo[t]
You have been warned!

LATRINES – What they are and why you should be careful when using them.

A BLIGHTY – What it is and how not to get one.

Soldiers made their own newsletters for their units.
They had jokes, and poked fun at life in the trenches.

Hygiene

35 Lice were one of the soldiers' main problems.   They laid their eggs along the seams in the soldiers' clothes, so the men would run a flame along the seams to pop the

40 eggs.   They called the lice 'chats', and popping the eggs, 'chatting'. Because they talked as they did this, this has given us our word 'chatting' today.

45 The men hated not being able to wash.   And they had to go to the toilet in pits dug into the sides of the trenches; a plank with holes cut into it was placed over the pit,

50 and the men had to sit there. The men did not just hate this because of the dirt and the smell. The Germans knew where the toilets were, and every now and

55 then they would fire a shell to kill anyone who was in there!

But the men could have a laugh too.   One thing they laughed at was the sausages – they called

60 them 'barkers' because they said they were made of dog-meat. And they called the army cheese 'bung', because they could not go to the toilet when they had

65 eaten it.

THINK ABOUT IT

Study Sources A and B with a friend. Using what you know about life in the trenches, make up your own fake adverts or funny stories.   Put your items with the others from your class to make up the fake soldiers' newsletter.

SOURCE B

BE IN THE FASHION.

Why have *Cats, Dogs, Canaries, Rabbits, Parrots, etc.?*

LICE !

EVERY CONCEIVABLE SHADE SUPPLIED :–BLUE BACKS, BLACK BACKS, RED BACKS, GREY BACKS, WHITE BACKS. ¶ ALSO IN A DELICATE PINK SHADE AND WITH VARIEGATED STRIPES. ¶ PURE THOROUGH-BREDS FROM OUR OWN SEAMS. ¶ MOST CLINGING, AFFECTIONATE, AND TAKING WAYS. ¶ VERY PROLIFIC, HARDY, AND WILL LIVE ANYWHERE. ¶ ONCE YOU HAVE THEM YOU WILL NEVER BE WITHOUT.

In Dainty Pochettes at 2/- per Thousand.

Write at once to E. R. M. CRACK,

Telegraphic Address : " Hitchy Koo."   CHAT VILLA, CRUMBY.

An advert for lice in a soldier's newsletter.

STOP AND REFLECT: If the conditions in the trenches were so bad, why did soldiers put up with them?   Think about:

- What happened to men who refused to fight.

- What other soldiers said about them.

Write a paragraph starting: 'Men kept on fighting because ...'

What was it like to fight in the war?

'Going over the top'

Sometimes, soldiers had to 'go over the top' of their trenches and run across '**no-man's-land**' (the strip of land in between the trenches) to
5 attack the enemy trenches.

A machine gun can fire 10 bullets a second. Both sides put down barbed wire to slow down attacking soldiers.   So the attackers were killed in vast numbers.

10 It was very bad waiting to go 'over the top'.   But once the attack started, many men said that they stopped being frightened.

SOURCE Ⓐ

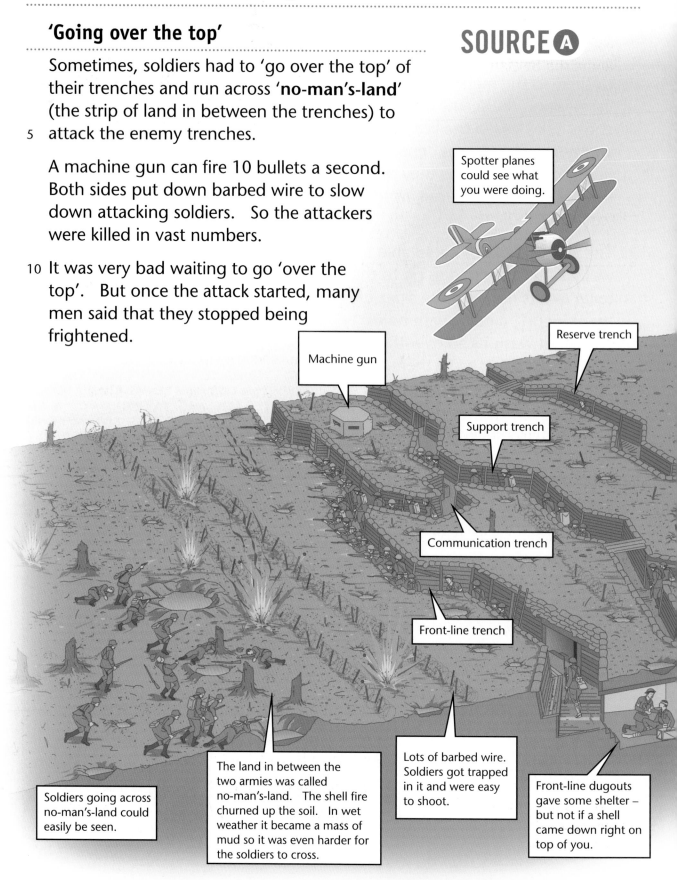

Spotter planes could see what you were doing.

Reserve trench

Machine gun

Support trench

Communication trench

Front-line trench

Soldiers going across no-man's-land could easily be seen.

The land in between the two armies was called no-man's-land.   The shell fire churned up the soil.   In wet weather it became a mass of mud so it was even harder for the soldiers to cross.

Lots of barbed wire. Soldiers got trapped in it and were easy to shoot.

Front-line dugouts gave some shelter – but not if a shell came down right on top of you.

STOP AND REFLECT:
Write a paragraph about the problems facing the British army.

SOURCE B

Norman Collins was an officer when he went over the top in the Battle of the Somme in 1916.

I knew that the men were watching me. They would not have thought much of me if I had shown that I was frightened. So I tried to cheer them up, and told them jokes. But I was very frightened. I just wanted to get through it alive.

After a battle, there were always men left out in no-man's-land. You could not save them, so they stayed there all night. But there was one thing you could do. They could die in agony or you could shoot them.

We knew how to do this. You put your gun to the back of the man's head and pulled the trigger. It blew out the man's brains. It did not hurt.

But I could not do it. You had to be brave to shoot a wounded soldier, and I was never brave enough to do it.

It is a good thing to shoot a friend who is wounded and in agony, but I was never brave enough to do it.

Norman Collins remembered this before he died, aged 100, in 1998.

Big guns – placed about 5 km behind the front line – could kill any soldiers who attacked.

If the enemy looked as if they were going to win, you could easily bring more men up to the front line.

A deep dugout. Some German dugouts were 15 metres underground – the German soldiers were safe there.

This picture shows why so many men died when they went 'over the top'.

THINK ABOUT IT

1. Look at Source A and think about why most attacks failed. Think about:
   - **What advantages did the defenders have?**
   - **What disadvantages did the attackers have?**

2. Norman Collins was only 19 in 1916! Scan Source B to find evidence that he:
   - **Tried to set a good example to his men.**
   - **Tried not to show fear.**
   - **Had to make difficult decisions.**
   - **Had to act older than his age.**

How far did the war affect the position of women? (1)

Today, women are equal to men. The law says that they should be able to do the same jobs as men and get the same wages.

5 Before 1914, things were different. Few rich women worked. A middle class woman might work as a teacher, but even she would give up her job when she got 10 married. People believed that a woman's job was to look after her husband.

Some women did not want this. They wanted to have a good job – like being a doctor. They wanted 15 to go to University.

Most of all, they wanted the vote. They said that, if women got the vote, then women would get into Parliament. And if they got into 20 Parliament, they said, women could change the laws to help women. Women who wanted the vote were called '**Suffragettes**'.

SOURCE A

Lillian Christofas (born in 1896) came from a middle class family. When her father tried to make her marry a rich man called Edward, Lillian asked her mother to try to stop him.

Well, she talked to my father, but she may as well have been talking to a brick wall. He said I had to marry Edward.

My mother said: 'This man is not the right man for her.' My father said: 'Be quiet. You do not know about these things.' He said that in front of me. My mother was very upset – *she wanted the ground to open up and swallow her.*

Edward came to visit and we went out for a walk. I had never been alone with him before. We walked across a field. When we had to get over a wall I made him turn round. I was wearing a long dress but I did not want him to see my legs.

During the wedding, I felt sick all the time. I was so sick I was not able to go away after the wedding. So we stayed in a hotel. We had different rooms, thank God. That was my first night as a wife in 1915.

The next day we went to London, and I had to be his wife. I went *like a lamb to the slaughter.* I knew nothing about sex and he was very over-sexed. I was scared and it hurt. It was like going to hell.

Edward went to fight in the Great War. He died and I was free.

Lillian's father found another husband for her, but she did not do as he told her. She married a Greek man. Her father hated him, but Lillian and he were very happy together until he died – 50 years later.

Lillian's memories, nearly 80 years later.

SOURCE B

SUFFRAGETTES
WHO HAVE NEVER
BEEN KISSED.

Not many men wanted women to have the vote. This postcard – drawn by a man – suggests women were Suffragettes because they could not get a husband.

THINK ABOUT IT

1. Lillian's mother 'wanted the ground to open up and swallow her' (a metaphor). And she says she went into marriage 'like a lamb to the slaughter' (a simile). What did she mean by these two phrases?

2. What does Source A tell you about:
   - how fathers treated their daughters,
   - how daughters treated their fathers,
   - how men treated their wives,
   - how wives treated their husbands?

3. Was Lillian ready for marriage in 1915?

4. What did Lillian mean by: 'he died and I was free'?

5. How are things different today?

STOP AND REFLECT:
Write paragraphs to explain:
- Why Lillian's father would have opposed the suffragettes.
- Why her mother may have opposed them.

How far did the war affect the position of women? (2)

SOURCE Ⓐ

Women war workers, 1917.

The war gave women the chance to DO things!

Women at war

From 1917, women joined the
5 armed forces – the army, the navy and the air force.   In all, about 100,000 women joined the armed forces.

(Right): In Source B, Mrs Martyn, a Suffragette, makes jam at home – even Suffragettes felt they needed to prove they could be 'good' wives and mothers.

Other women went to the war as nurses.   One British nurse, Edith Cavell, was shot by the Germans because she helped British soldiers get back to Britain. 10

The Home Front

The Suffragettes stopped trying to get the vote.   Instead they tried to help the war effort.   At first, the government told women to stay at home.   But as more and more men went off to fight, the government was happy for women to take up 'war work'. 15 20

By 1918, 900,000 women were working making shells and bullets. The work was dangerous – it turned their skin yellow and gave them cancer. 25

Other women did men's jobs – such as driving trams and buses, and becoming policewomen. 30

But one thing did not change.   The women workers got much less pay than the men who had done these jobs before the war.

SOURCE B

THINK ABOUT IT

Describe the situation for women before the war, then list the changes during and after the war.
How important were the changes?

After the war
35

In December 1918, women aged 30 or over got the right to vote. In 1919, women who got married were given the right to carry on working.
40

But some things did not get better. Women over 21 did not get the vote until 1928, and women teachers who married were forced to give up their jobs until 1944.
45

And even today, many fewer women hold top jobs than men.

STOP AND REFLECT: Write a paragraph starting: 'The Great War helped women get the vote because ...'

Pulling it Together

How did the First World War change British society?

Make spidergrams of what you have learned about how the war affected:

- The Soldiers – conditions in the trenches, and what they had to do.

- The Conscientious Objectors – how people treated them, and what happened to them.

- Women – how their lives changed, and how some things improved as a result of the war.

Pretend to be one of these groups of people and make a presentation of 'how the war changed your life'.

You could:

- Write an imaginary letter to a friend, or

- Give a speech to the class, describing the effect that the war had upon you.

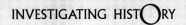

CHAPTER 2

The Nazi Dictatorship
Why was Hitler so popular in Germany?

In this chapter you will:

- Study why the German people liked Hitler.
- Find out how he got Germans to support him.
- Think about who gained and who lost from Nazi rule.
- Learn why Hitler got his way in Europe.

How did the defeat of 1918 help Hitler?

The 'Stab in the Back'

Germany was defeated in the First World War.   Germany just had too many enemies – Britain, France and
5 America.   After March 1918, the German army was slowly driven back and, on 11 November 1918, the German government agreed to stop fighting (the '**Armistice**').

10 However, the German army did not *feel* that it had been defeated. It had not run away.   Many soldiers had been willing to go on fighting.   They said the men who
15 had signed the Armistice had 'stabbed them in the back', and called them 'the November criminals'.   One of these soldiers, a man called Adolf Hitler, later
20 became the **dictator** of Germany.

SOURCE A

Just 4 days before the Armistice, the Germans seemed to have lots more fight left in them:

The Germans are defending very well.   They have lots of time to set up new machine-gun posts, and lots of men are killed every time we attack.   Everyone thinks that the Germans can go on fighting for half a year or more.

Written by a British army priest, 7 November 1918.

THINK ABOUT IT

1. Explain the 'stab in the back' theory in your own words.
2. Does Source A suggest that this theory was right, or mistaken?

SOURCE B

Map of Germany after the Treaty of Versailles.

How did the Treaty of Versailles help the Nazis?

After the war, Britain, France and America made the Germans agree to the Treaty of Versailles.
25 This was VERY harsh on the Germans.

It said:
- Germany was to blame for the war.
- Germany had to give away lots of land (where lots of German people lived).
30 - Germany had to pay nearly £7 billion to pay for ALL the damage done during the war.
- Germany could not have an army of more than 100,000 men, or a navy of more than six ships.

The German people 35 HATED the Treaty of Versailles. They said it was not fair.

Hitler said that – if he ever got into 40 power – he would tear up the Treaty of Versailles. The German people loved him when he 45 said this.

Was the Treaty too harsh?

Some people said that Hitler was right 50 – that the Treaty WAS too harsh. They said that Germany would never be able to pay £7 billion because it 55 had to give away so much land and so many people.

But some people said that the Treaty was 60 NOT too harsh – America lent Germany most of the money to pay, and Germany became 65 very rich in the 1920s.

But whether the Treaty was too harsh or not, it made the Germans angry, and 70 in this way it helped to cause World War Two.

The Rhineland. The German army could not go here – it was next to France.

The Polish Corridor. This land – and all the Germans who lived there – was given to Poland. East Prussia was cut off from the rest of Germany.

DENMARK

EAST PRUSSIA

HOLLAND

GERMANY

BELGIUM

POLAND

N

Alsace-Lorraine: returned to France.

CZECHOSLOVAKIA

SWITZERLAND

AUSTRIA

0   km   500

FRANCE

Austria. Seven million Germans lived here. They could not unite with Germany.

The Sudetenland. This land – and the 3 million Germans who lived there – was given to Czechoslovakia.

How did Hitler persuade Germans to support him?

Economic problems: savings and jobs

In 1923, prices went up and up. A loaf of bread that had cost a few marks went up until it cost trillions of marks. This is called '**hyper-inflation**'. People who had saved a little

5 money lost everything – their savings would not even buy them a loaf of bread. The government did not know what to do. People were

10 very angry with the government.

In 1929, things went wrong again. This time prices fell.

15 Many firms went bust. This is called 'the Great **Depression**'. Many people lost their jobs,

20 and then their homes. They lost everything and their children were hungry.

25 When people are very poor, they get very angry. People who have lost everything have

30 nothing to lose.

Some German people turned to the Communists. But many people turned

35 to Hitler.

SOURCE Ⓐ

In 1923 the price of toys went up so high that no one could buy building bricks. So they made bricks out of bank-notes. It shows how worthless money had become.

Hitler's attack on democracy

Hitler was a good speaker. His words
40 were full of hate. He told the German people what they wanted to hear.

He said:

45 • Germany is great and Germans are better than other people.

• Germany did not
50 lose the war – the government stabbed us in the back.

• First hyper-inflation, now the
55 Great Depression – we are poor and hungry because the government is useless.

60 • Communists will take over soon.

• Things will get better if you give me power.

65 Many people turned to Hitler. What had they to lose?

THINK ABOUT IT

In November 1932, the Germans had an election to elect a new government. We know now that Hitler was only 2 months away from getting power in Germany (in January 1933).

Make up a speech such as Hitler might have given in 1932.

The speech will have FIVE sections, in which it will explain the things that Hitler told the German people. Some ideas have been added to help you:

- Germany is great and Germans are better than other people.
  (You could point out that Germany had fought for 4 years, and had defeated Russia.)
- Germany did not lose the war – the government stabbed us in the back.
  (Source A on page 20 thought they still had lots of fight left in them.)
- First hyper-inflation, now the Great Depression: we are poor and hungry because the government is useless.
  (Page 22 will help here.)
- Communists will take over soon.
  (Many people were frightened the Communists would take away the money of the rich.)
- Things will get better if you give me power.
  (Finish by asking people to vote for the Nazi Party.)

STOP AND REFLECT: Write two paragraphs starting:
'Germany had two ecomonic disasters in the 1920s and 1930s … [Describe them.]
'This helped Hitler come to power because …'

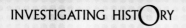

Who benefited from Hitler's rule?

SOURCE Ⓐ

A German farmer's wife, Luise Essig, remembers going to see Hitler:

Thousands of farmers and young people came from all over Germany.   They walked miles and waited hours just to get a place at the front.   They wanted to say 'thank you' to him for everything he had done for them.   Things were looking up.   No man has ever been as loved as Hitler was then.   It's all coming back to me!   Those were happy times!

SOURCE Ⓑ

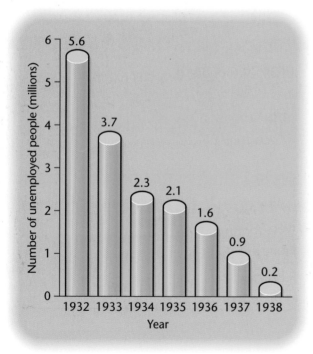

Unemployment levels in Germany, 1932–1938.

Millions voted Nazi

Hitler did not take power by force. He was given power in 1933 because the Nazis were the biggest party in Germany.   In the 1932 elections, 14 million Germans – 37% of the people – voted Nazi.   Lots of people liked the Nazi Party. [5]

- Most farmers voted Nazi. [10]

- Middle class people, and people who owned small firms, often voted Nazi.

- Office workers voted Nazi.

- At first, most factory workers voted Communist, but soon they changed to vote Nazi. [15]

Hitler spent billions of marks on Germany's army – in 1933 the government spent 3 billion marks on the armed forces; by 1938 this had grown to 17 billion marks, six times as much.   This gave more work to the coal mines, the steel mills and the iron workers.   The economy boomed, and there were millions of new jobs (see Source B). [20] [25]

There was lots of money about, and everybody was very happy with Hitler's government. [30]

SOURCE ⊙

A Nazi Party rally in 1938. You can see that the people really loved Hitler.

Propaganda

Hitler thought of other ways to make people happy – there were
35 free trips and holidays, although few people ever got to go on one.

Then, in 1936, Hitler held the Olympic Games in Berlin.   Not only were the Games a happy
40 time, but Germany won more gold medals than any other country (33 – the USA only won 24).   This helped Hitler's claim that the Germans were better than other
45 races like Jews and black people.

THINK ABOUT IT

1. The man in charge of Nazi propaganda was Josef Goebbels. Goebbels used films to get Nazi ideas across to people.

Your task is to plan a short Nazi propaganda film – based on Sources A–D – about how good the Nazis are.

The ideas at the top of page 27 will help you write the commentary to go with the pictures.

SOURCE D

The 100 m sprint in the 1936 Olympics was won by Jessie Owens (on the right). Owens won four gold medals.   This made Hitler angry, because Owens was black.

Scene One	An interview with Luise Essig, farmer's wife (Source A on page 24). Luise has asked you to write down for her what she has to say on camera; make up two questions for the interviewer to ask her, and the answers you want her to give.
Scene Two	The film will show a graph of unemployment in Germany, 1932–38 (Source B on page 24). Finish the narrator's voiceover, which starts: 'Millions have found work since we took over. In 1932 six million Germans were without work. Now …'
Scene Three	The film shows scenes of the 1938 rally (Source C on page 25). The narrator will say four sentences all beginning: 'See how …'
Scene Four	The film finishes with scenes of the Olympic Games. What will the narrator say about the Games? Explain what part of Source D will have to be cut out of the film and why.

Women and girls

The Nazis believed that a woman's place was in the home, looking after the children.   They gave
50 mothers money for the first 4 babies they had.   Mothers who had 8 or more children got a gold medal on 12 August – the birthday of Hitler's mother.
55 Pregnant women were told not to slim or to smoke, so their babies would be strong.   The Nazis did not like women to perm their hair, wear trousers or put on make-up.

60 Girls did not do the same work at school as the boys.   They had to keep fit – fit girls would have strong babies.   They learned things that would make them
65 good mothers.   Not all girls were happy about this – they called their Cookery exam 'the Pudding level'.

THINK ABOUT IT

2. Suppose the people of Britain elected a leader like Adolf Hitler. Would it be right for a foreign power to try to stop him becoming leader? Talk about this with your class.

STOP AND REFLECT: Think about why the Germans supported Hitler, then finish these sentences:
- Hitler helped the workers because …
- Hitler increased the armed forces so …
- The Olympic Games helped because…

27

SOURCE Ⓐ

Maths Question 95

It costs 6 million marks to build a hospital for lunatics. How many houses at 15,000 marks could have been built for that money?

Maths Question 97

To keep a mentally ill person costs 4 marks a day. A disabled person costs $5\frac{1}{2}$ marks, a prisoner $3\frac{1}{2}$ marks. Many workers get only 4 marks a day wage.

a. Draw a graph to show this.

b. There are 300,000 mentally ill people in Germany. How much do they cost to keep in total?

Questions from a Nazi school Maths textbook.

Who suffered under Nazi rule?

Everything was used to get the Nazi message over to people – even Maths lessons were used to teach children to hate mentally ill people. It was more important that they learned that than that they learned Maths.

5

The Nazis said that the Jews were behind Communism.

The artist mocks Jewish faces by drawing thick lips, a big nose and straggly beard.

The Nazis said that Jews were greedy.

SOURCE Ⓑ

This Nazi propaganda picture shows a Jew as both a bad businessman AND a Communist. Pictures like this made many German people hate the Jews.

The Nazis said that Jewish businessmen made their wokers work like slaves.

Hitler's hate list

Hitler wanted all Germans to hate.
10 The hate-list was a long one.

Mentally ill and disabled people cost money and made the German people weak.   Nazis believed that they had to be killed.

15 The Nazis thought that Germans were better than other peoples. Most of all, they hated black people and the Jews, but they also hated the Russians and the
20 gypsies.

Then the Nazis added other people to hate – Communists, priests, homosexuals and **pacifists**.

The Nazis hated the Jews more
25 than anybody else.   Jewish people had been hated in many countries since the Middle Ages, and this made Hitler's job easy.   The Nazis treated the Jews badly for many
30 years in Germany.   But in 1941, the Nazis started to mass-murder the Jews.   They wanted to wipe the Jews off the face of the earth. This mass-murder is called the
35 **Holocaust**.

Boycott

The Nazis hated the fact that many Jews were rich.   On 1 April 1933, the Nazis told the German
40 people to **boycott** (stay away from) shops owned by Jewish people.   They passed laws to stop Jews being doctors or lawyers.

The Jews knew what was happening.   They wanted to get 45 out of Germany – even though they had to hand over their homes and businesses.   Many countries said that they did not want any Jews to go and live there.   But 50 by 1941, three-quarters of Germany's Jews had left Germany – 100,000 went to America and 50,000 went to live in Britain.

The Nuremberg Laws
55
Some Jews stayed in Germany. They hoped that things would get better.   But they were wrong.   As time went on, things got worse for the Jews in Germany. 60

In 1935, Hitler passed the Nuremberg Laws.   These said that:

● Jews could not marry Germans.

● Jews could not be German citizens. 65

● Jews could not use public baths or parks.

Most Germans did not care about what was happening to the Jews. In fact, many Germans seemed 70 happy to see bad things happening to the Jews.   After 1938, Jewish people were told to hand over their businesses to Germans – and many Germans were very happy 75 to take over from them.

The Night of Broken Glass

Early in November 1938, in Paris, a Jewish man killed a German. On
80 the night of 9 November 1938, the Nazis in Germany attacked the German Jews. They smashed the windows of Jewish shops – they called it 'the night of broken glass'.
85 The police were told to do nothing.

91 Jews were killed. 30,000 Jewish men were sent to work camps – although most were sent
90 home soon after, about 1,000 Jews were killed in the camps.

Mass killing begins

Hitler wanted the Germans to become the '**master-race**'. He wanted them to be perfect. There 95 was no place in Hitler's Germany for anyone who was sick or weak.

After 1939, the Nazis began to kill Germans who were disabled or mentally ill. They gassed them. 100 Between 1939 and 1941, 70,000 disabled Germans were killed.

In 1941 a Catholic priest found out what the Nazis were doing. People were angry with the government. 105 For a short time, the Nazis stopped the killing, but then they started again in secret.

SOURCE G

How the Nazis attacked the Jews, 1933–1939.

Why didn't Germans oppose Hitler?

110

Hitler was a wicked man, but the Germans loved him.   Why was this?

One reason was because Hitler attacked small groups – only 1% of the German people were Jews. Another reason was that, if you said anything against Hitler, you were put in prison or killed.   It was safer to look the other way.

115

120

Most of all, many Germans were well off when Hitler was in power. They were happy.   One woman still alive today says: 'It was a good time.   I liked it … there was law and order.'   Most Germans were happy just to enjoy the good things about Nazi Germany.

125

SOURCE E

In December 1938, a Jewish family told the police that three drunken Nazis had stolen some things from their home.

After a few hours, the police came.   We told them what had happened and who did it. The men were sent to prison for a long time.

People could only attack the Jews when the government told them to.

SOURCE D

A Nazi painting showing the perfect family.

THINK ABOUT IT

1. Write a sentence about each of the events shown in Source C.

2. What were the questions in Source A (page 28) trying to teach German children?

3. Why is the story in Source E surprising?   Why were the three men put in prison?

4. What made the family in Source D the 'perfect family' for the Nazis?

5. Are there any groups of people in Britain today who are treated badly? Why?

STOP AND REFLECT: Think about why the Germans let Hitler do these things, then write a sentence starting:

'The Germans did not stop Hitler attacking the Jews because …'

Why did Hitler get his way in Europe?

SOURCE Ⓐ

This is what happened when a 14-year-old girl shook Hitler's hand:

'He came. Everything got quiet and we were so happy. When he came to me I nearly forgot to give him my hand; I just looked at him and I saw good eyes. I said to myself: "I will always follow you because you are a good man" – and I did.'

So far we have looked at what Hitler did to people in Germany. Now we will look at what he did to other countries – this made the German people love him even more.

SOURCE Ⓑ

Daladier, the Prime Minister of France.

This cartoon was drawn by David Low, a British cartoonist who hated Hitler. He is saying that Hitler had fooled the leaders of Britain, France and Italy into doing what he wanted.

A British Lord.

Neville Chamberlain, British Prime Minister.

Mussolini, leader of Italy.

5 Hitler's attack on the Treaty of Versailles

Hitler hated the Treaty of Versailles. He wanted to get rid of it. After 1935, he made the German army bigger and bigger. This broke the
10 Treaty of Versailles, but Britain and France did nothing.

Then, in 1935, Britain agreed to let Germany have a bigger navy. Yet again, Hitler had broken the Treaty of Versailles – but this time he had 15 been helped by Britain. Hitler said it was the happiest day of his life!

The Treaty of Versailles said that the German army could not go into the Rhineland – the part of 20 Germany next to France. In March 1936, Hitler sent 3,000 German soldiers into the Rhineland. They had orders to run away if the French army tried to stop them. 25 But France and Britain did nothing – yet again, they let Hitler get away with it.

Austria united with Germany

The people of Austria were 30 Germans by race. In 1938, the German army marched into Austria and took over. Then Hitler held a vote – 99% of the Austrians voted to be part of Germany. 35

Neville Chamberlain had become Prime Minister of Britain in 1937. He hated war, and he did not want a war with Germany. So Britain and France did nothing – 40 they let Hitler take over.

Low shows Hitler pretending to be good.

People are being given their voting papers already filled in!

There is no box for votes against Hitler.

Josef Goebbels, in charge of Hitler's propaganda.

Czechoslovakia disappears

Hitler said that he wanted to get all the Germans in Europe into one
45 country, into what he called 'Greater Germany'. Hitler now turned to Czechoslovakia.

3 million Germans lived in Czechoslovakia, in the land next to
50 Germany called the 'Sudetenland'. But Czechoslovakia did not want Hitler to get the Sudetenland. Czechoslovakia had a good army and – with a little help – could
55 have stopped Hitler.

Czechoslovakia thought Britain and France would help against Hitler. But Neville Chamberlain did not want a war with Germany. Hitler
60 said that he did not want any more land in Europe – and Chamberlain believed him. In September 1938, at Munich in Germany, Britain, France and Italy GAVE the
65 Sudetenland to Hitler. Czechoslovakia was not consulted!

In March 1939, Hitler broke his promise. The German army took over the rest of Czechoslovakia.
70 Soon after, Hitler said that he wanted to take over those parts of Poland where Germans were living.

Chamberlain now saw that Hitler would only be stopped by a war.
75 He promised Poland that Britain would help if Germany attacked Poland.

SOURCE C

This is what a British newspaper said when Chamberlain came back from Munich on 1 October 1938.

He went from the plane to see the King, and he came out with the King and Queen to wave to the crowds.

Everyone shouted 'Neville!' when he waved to them. This went on for 3 minutes.

Then he went to Downing Street. There were more crowds there. Everywhere there were people cheering. One woman there said this: 'This is the man who gave me back my son.'

SOURCE D

Nazi–Soviet Pact

80 Hitler thought that Chamberlain was too weak to keep his promise to Poland. But he DID think that Russia might help Poland against him. Communist Russia and Nazi Germany hated each other.

85 So, in August 1939, Germany made a Pact (an agreement) with Russia not to fight each other. The rest of the world was shocked! Secretly, Russia and Germany also 90 agreed to attack Poland and split it between them.

Now Hitler was free to attack Poland, which he did on 1 September 1939. Two days 95 later, Britain declared war on Germany – the Second World War had begun.

Chamberlain waves to the crowds cheering him, 1 October, 1938.

THINK ABOUT IT

1. Look at Sources C and D. Did the British want war in 1938?

2. What did the woman in Source C mean by 'the man who gave me back my son'? (What would have happened to her son if there had been a war.)

3. Do Sources C and D help explain why Chamberlain gave way to Hitler?

4. Some people say that Chamberlain caused the Second World War. They say that – by not standing up to Hitler – he LET Hitler go on until there had to be a war to stop him.

Talk about this as a class. Include these ideas in your discussion:
- Britain and France could easily have stopped Hitler increasing his army or invading the Rhineland.
- The British government gave way to Hitler long before Chamberlain became Prime Minister.
- The French government gave way to Hitler too.
- The British PEOPLE did not want war.

STOP AND REFLECT: Write a paragraph starting:
'The Germans loved Hitler's foreign policy because …'

Pulling it Together

Why was Hitler so popular in Germany?

We know now that Hitler was a bad man.   But the German people at the time loved him.   This chapter has been about trying to understand why the German people loved Hitler.

You are going to write an essay about why Hitler was so popular in Germany.   This will be a formal piece of discursive writing in four paragraphs.

Help with the essay

1. Look at the question.   It is asking you WHY something happened, so you know that your answer will have to say '*because ...*'   You will need to find and write about the *reasons* why Hitler was popular.

2. You will need some ideas to put in the essay to explain why Hitler was popular.   If you follow these instructions, they will help you think of FOUR reasons why the German people loved Hitler.

   a. Split the class into four groups, to look at pages 20–21, pages 22–23, pages 24–27, and pages 32–35.

   b. Each group of pupils will read their pages and make a list of key words.   They will look back in their notes to see what they wrote for the **Stop and Reflect** exercise at the end of their section.   And they will talk about what made the German people love Hitler.

   c. After a while, come back together. The class will have FOUR reasons why the Germans loved Hitler:

   - because they hated the Treaty of Versailles (pages 20–21).

   - because they were poor (pages 22–23).

   - because his government gave them things they wanted (pages 24–27).

   - because he made Germany a great world power again (pages 32–35).

   d. Ask each group in turn to share the key words they collected, and to explain how it was that each thing made the German people love Hitler.   The teacher can collect the ideas and write them on the board.

3. Now you are ready to write the essay. You will write four paragraphs – one for each reason. Each paragraph will have:

    a. A Statement ('One reason the Germans loved Hitler was because …').

    b. Evidence (some facts you have found out).

    c. Explanation (WHY this made them love Hitler).

This writing frame will help you write your essay:

Paragraph 1	
Starter:	**Copy this:** 'The first reason the Germans loved Hitler was because they hated the Treaty of Versailles.'
Evidence	**Write in your own words about:** the 'stab in the back' and the harsh terms of the Treaty of Versailles.
Explanation	**Explain in your own words** why the German people loved Hitler when he said that – if he ever got into power – he would tear up the Treaty of Versailles.
Paragraph 2	
Starter:	**Copy this:** 'The second reason the Germans loved Hitler was because they were poor.'
Evidence	**Write in your own words about** hyper-inflation and the Great Depression.
Explanation	**Explain in your own words** why all this made people support Hitler. Ideas that will help you include the fact that the Germans had nothing to lose, and that they were afraid that the Communists might take over.
Paragraph 3	
Starter:	**Copy this:** 'The third reason the Germans loved Hitler was because his government gave them things.'
Evidence	**Write in your own words about** spending on the army / The booming economy / Free trips and holidays / the Olympic Games.
Explanation	**Explain in your own words** why this made the Germans love him. Talk about how Josef Goebbels used propaganda. You might also mention Luise Essig or the 14-year-old girl on page 32.
Paragraph 4	
Starter:	**Copy this:** 'The fourth reason the Germans loved Hitler was because he made Germany a great world power again.'
Evidence	**Write in your own words about** how Hitler increased the army, then marched into the Rhineland, Austria, the Sudetenland and Czechoslovakia.
Explanation	**Explain in your own words** why all this made people support Hitler. Include the idea that Hitler made Germans believe they were better than other peoples.

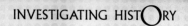

CHAPTER 3

Revolution!

Did the Russian Revolution really make life better for ordinary Russians?

In this chapter you will:

- Find out why the Russians revolted against their Tsar.
- Learn why they then had a second revolution.
- Learn why there was a Civil War.
- Find out how Stalin changed Russia.
- Think about whether the Russian revolution made life better or worse.

SOURCE A

A British nurse went to help the Russians. This is what she saw:

A young soldier came to the hospital. He was upset because the army was losing the war. He blamed the generals.

He said: 'They do not understand how tired we are. They sit in their hotels far from the fighting and point to a map and say, we must take that place. And then our men – hungry, cold and tired to death – have to jump up and attack that place, no matter how many of them die doing so.'

Written by a nurse who was in Russia during the war.

In 1917, Russia had TWO revolutions. In the first revolution, the people of Russia got rid of their ruler (called the **Tsar**). The second revolution turned Russia into a Communist country. 5

Before the First World War, Russia was ruled by Tsar Nicholas II. Many Russians loved him. Few people said anything bad about the government – Nicholas was a dictator, and anybody who said anything bad about him 10 was sent to a prison camp.

Collapse in Russia

The First World War changed things in Russia.

When the war broke out, many Russians had been very happy. But the war went badly for 15 Russia. Nearly 2 million Russian soldiers were killed. By 1916 the Russians knew they were going to lose the war. They blamed the government for this.

Shortages

Back in Russia, things were going wrong as well. The army was taking all the food to feed the soldiers, and all the coal to power the railways. The Russian people went hungry and cold in the freezing Russian winter.

By March 1917, they had had enough. They went on protest marches. The Tsar sent his soldiers, but the soldiers joined the marchers.

They forced the Tsar to give up the throne.

SOURCE B

Russian women line up for bread. The people turned against the Tsar because they were hungry.

SOURCE C

The Tsar's son, Alexei, was a sickly child. The only person who could help him was a holy man called Rasputin.

But Rasputin was a drunkard. People said that he and the Tsarina (the Tsar's wife) were lovers. They hated him, and they hated the Tsarina.

Rasputin was killed in 1916 – though his killers had to poison, shoot and drown him before he died.

THINK ABOUT IT

1. How did the war affect:
   a) the soldiers (Source A)
   b) the people back home (Source B)

2. How did Rasputin change the way people thought about the Tsar (Source C).

3. Write a paragraph starting: 'The Russians turned against the Tsar in 1917 for three reasons …'

Why did Russia have another revolution?

New government, old mistakes

The March Revolution threw out the Tsar. But Kerensky, the leader of the new government which
5 took over from the Tsar, wanted to go on with the war. This meant that the people still had great hardship; they were still poor and hungry.

10 Kerensky thought that the soldiers would fight better under a new government. He was wrong. The Russian army was defeated again and again. The soldiers
15 started to go home. They did not follow their orders. Instead, they set up soldiers' meetings called '**Soviets**' and gave themselves their own orders.

20 In the towns, the workers also set up Soviets – they did not obey the government, but made laws for themselves.

All this gave a chance to a small
25 revolutionary group called the '**Bolsheviks**'. The Bolsheviks were extreme Communists. Their leader was a man called Lenin.

The Bolsheviks wanted to throw
30 Kerensky from power and take over the government.

SOURCE A

Women can fight. Women are brave enough and strong enough for war. The Russians have shown us that women can fight.

Written by an American woman. The women in the Russian army were the only women's unit in the First World War.

Peace, Bread, Land

Lenin's cry was 'Peace, Bread, Land'. He said that if the war ended, then food would start to come into 35 the towns. And then he would take the land from the rich and give it to the poor people (who made up 80% of the population).

The Russians loved Lenin when he 40 said this. In June 1917, 11% of the people voted for the Bolsheviks. In September, 51% voted for them.

All the time, the Bolsheviks were plotting revolution. Kerensky 45 knew, but he could do nothing. On the night of 6 November, the Red Guards (the Bolshevik army) took over the bridges and the telephones. The next night they 50 were ready to take over the country.

The Bolshevik Revolution

The only soldiers left who wanted
55 to fight for Kerensky were boys
and women – they did not put up
a good fight.   The Red Guards
easily defeated them.   Kerensky
got away, but the other
60 government leaders were put in
prison.   Lenin took over as the
new leader of Russia.

Lenin gave the people what he
had promised.   In December 1917
65 he stopped the fighting, and in
March 1918 he made peace with
Germany.   Food began to get into
the towns.   And Lenin passed laws
to give the poor people their own
land.   70

Lenin also set up a Soviet for the
whole country – but it did not last
long.   A civil war started in Russia
as Lenin's enemies tried to throw
him out of power.   Lenin sent the   75
Soviet home and ran the
government himself.

SOURCE B

*There were about
140 women
defending
Kerensky's
government.
They were taken
prisoner, but
later the Bolsheviks
set them free.*

SOURCE C

The events of 1914–1917

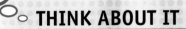

THINK ABOUT IT

Use the information in this chapter to write a recount of the events of 1914–1917.

1. Source C shows, in picture form, EIGHT events in the story of the Russian revolutions (in the wrong order). Source D has the captions (also out of order). Choose the right captions for the pictures in Source C, and sort the EIGHT events into the right order.

2. Tell the story of the Russian revolutions using the captions in Source D.

   a) FIRST, list the captions in the correct order.

   b) THEN, change the tense of the captions from present tense to past tense (for example, 'In 1914 the people *are* happy to go to war for the Tsar.' will become 'In 1914 the people *were* happy to go to war for the Tsar.').

   c) NEXT, use connectives (words such as 'but', 'and', 'so', 'therefore', 'however' and 'also') to join some of the phrases together so that your whole text comprises just three or four sentences.

   d) FINALLY, read out your text to the class to show that it forms a continuous narrative.

SOURCE D

a) *The Russians go on protest marches against the Tsar, March 1917.*

b) *The people in the towns are hungry.*

c) *Millions of Russian soldiers are killed in battle.*

d) *The people in the towns are STILL hungry.*

e) *The new government under Kerensky tries to carry on the war.*

f) *In 1914 the people are happy to go to war for the Tsar.*

g) *The Tsar gives up the throne and stops ruling Russia.*

h) *Lenin and the Bolsheviks are able to overthrow Kerensky.*

STOP AND REFLECT: Think about why Russia had a Bolshevik revolution, then write a paragraph starting: 'Lenin came to power in Russia in November 1917 because …'

What kind of war was the Russian Civil War?

After 1917, the followers of the Tsar (called the 'Whites') tried to get rid of the
5 Communists (called the 'Reds'). There was a civil war (1918–1920). Both sides did terrible
10 things.

This story is from a German newspaper of 1919. It tells how the Whites killed
15 some Communist soldiers they had captured.

SOURCE Ⓐ

The Whites ask every soldier if he is a Communist and they hang or shoot every one who says yes. The Reds know this.

The captured soldiers are told: 'If you are Communists and are brave enough, step forward.' Slowly, sticking together, about half the men step forward. They are told they will be shot. But before they die, they have to dig their own graves.

The Reds are told to take off their clothes. The Whites need them, and they do not want them to be covered with blood. The Reds slowly take off their clothes and put them in a pile to one side.

It is night. The Reds stand there in the moonlight. Their skin looks white – even see-through. They begin to dig big graves. There is a tear in every eye. They keep digging. It is getting darker and darker.

At last the graves are deep enough. Have any of them any last wishes? Even though every one of them has a wife and children at home, only one or two take off their rings and hand them in to be sent home to their family.

I ask one of them: 'Why did you become a Communist?' He says: 'Because I am so poor. Life should be happy.'

The Whites have their guns ready to shoot. The Reds line up, like a white wall in the moonlight. 'Fire' – there is a flash and the crack of guns. The Reds are still standing. Another bang. The bullets hit them; thick blood leaps into the air. Some are not dead. They cry out – I feel sick. The guns fire again and again. Some who are still alive cry out: 'Kill us!'. One man puts his hand on his heart and shouts: 'Shoot here!'

At last, they are all dead. They are in a pile next to the graves. It is all over. It is quiet.

Written by a Russian who fought for the 'Whites'.

SOURCE ⓑ

White soldiers stand by the bodies of 'Reds' they have just shot.

THINK ABOUT IT

1. The writer of Source A was a White. Did he hate the Reds? Which parts of the Source show that he felt pity for the Reds?

2. How did the Reds meet their deaths (were they brave, for instance)?

3. Does Source B prove that there were lots of killings like in Source A?

4. Re-write Source A as if you were a supporter of the Reds. Re-write it paragraph by paragraph. Write it in such a way – using strong words and feelings – to show how heartless, cruel and pitiless the Whites were.

The civil war was terrible. Many killings were not as quick as the ones in Source A. The Reds did worse things than the Whites. Also, the poor people wanted the Reds to win. So, in the end, the Reds won.   20

Lenin died, and in 1924 Josef Stalin became the leader of Russia. He had learned that you can win if you kill all your enemies.   25

STOP AND REFLECT: Write a paragraph starting: 'The Communists won the Civil War because ...'

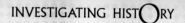

How did Stalin change the Soviet Union?

Agriculture

Stalin knew that Russia was backward. He wanted the farmers to produce more food. His plan
5 was to join all the peasants' small farms into one big farm for each village. This was called **'collectivisation'**. Peasants who didn't agree were killed.

10 The rich peasants (called **'kulaks'**) were angry about losing their land. They burned their crops and killed their animals. Because of this there was a **famine** in the 1930s.

Industry

15

Stalin wanted the factories to make more. His plans were called the 'Five Year Plans' – they set targets for how much steel, coal and oil he wanted to be produced. 20 Workers were made to work long hours. If they did not meet their targets, they were punished or killed.

By 1939, Russia produced a lot of 25 steel, coal and oil, but little was produced of the things people needed – like clothes and houses.

SOURCE Ⓐ

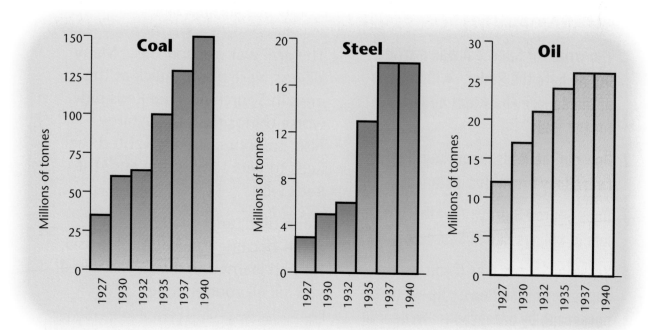

What Russia produced 1927–1940 (millions of tonnes)

SOURCE B

Starving Russian children. 5 million Russians died in a famine after the Civil War and 5 million more people died during the famine of the 1930s.

SOURCE C

This is what a modern historian has found out about what Stalin did to the farmers. It is based on what people of the time said.

Stalin's men went everywhere. They broke into the houses, smashed them up, and took everything – food, clothes, tools, tables, chairs … Many people – who knew that this was going to happen – had sold their things and killed their animals. One woman set fire to her home. She shouted: 'I have worked all my life for this home. You will not have it. The fire shall have it!'

When you went into a village there was no noise. The people said: 'We've eaten all the dogs – all the cats, mice and birds. We've even eaten the bark from the trees.'

Stalin did not care. Men were sent to stop the peasants going into the towns to beg for food. When one Red Army soldier saw an old woman and two dying children, he would not let aid workers help them. He said: 'They do not want to work. They are kulaks. They are the enemies of Russia.'

Written by a modern historian in 1985.

THINK ABOUT IT

1. What evidence is there in Source C that people were starving?

2. Why did the government say that the kulaks were to blame for the famine?

3. Look at Source D.   How do we know that the artist did not see the shooting?

4. Can we trust Source D?   To decide this, you need to think about:
   - Does the picture fit with what we know about the event?
   - Is there anything in the picture which you do not believe?

SOURCE D

Lev Karakhan was killed in 1937.   He would not admit that he was plotting against Stalin – so Stalin's secret police just shot him in secret.   This painting, from Italy in 1938, was drawn by a man who hated the Communists.

The Terror

Stalin knew that many people were not happy in Russia.   He thought that they were plotting to get rid of him. [30]

So he killed them.

Top of his list were the other members of the Communist government.   After 1936 he got rid of them.   They were put on trial and killed.   Stalin even killed the man in charge of the killings! [35] [40]

Nobody was safe.   Stalin killed 3 million people.   He sent 2 million more to work camps (where they died of the cold).   Stalin wanted everybody to be afraid that they would be next. [45]

Nobody stood up to Stalin because they were afraid of what he would do to their families. Instead, everybody said all the time how much they loved Stalin! [50]

STOP AND REFLECT: Write a sentence each about Collectivisation, the Five Year Plans and The Terror.

Pulling it Together

Did the Russian Revolution really make life better for ordinary Russians?

When the Communists took over Russia in 1917 they said they were doing so to make people's lives better.

But did it?   To decide this, you need to compare life BEFORE the Revolution with life AFTER the Revolution.   Really it's a case of from bad to bad, isn't it?   But was it *worse* bad, or *not-as-bad* bad under Stalin?

1. FIRST, read pages 38–39 to see what life was like before the revolution.   Make a spidergram of the good things and the bad things.   Think about:

   - How rich people were.

   - What the government was like.

2. NEXT, read pages 46–48 to look at life under Stalin. Make a spidergram of the good and bad things. Concentrate on:

   - How rich people were.

   - What the government was like.

3. Finally, use your spidergrams to write an essay in three paragraphs, starting:

   a) 'Before the Russian revolution, life …' (then describe what it was like).

   b) 'Under Stalin, life …' (then describe what it was like).

   c) 'Overall, I think that life got better / worse.   I say this because …' (and explain why you think that).

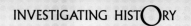

CHAPTER 4

American Dream, or Nightmare?

Did the New Deal save America from Depression?

In this chapter you will:

- **Find out what happened in America in the Depression of the 1930s.**
- **See how it affected one 15-year-old girl.**
- **Learn that some rich Americans were not affected at all.**
- **Think about how successful Roosevelt was in ending the Depression.**

The 1920s had been good times for most Americans, but in the 1930s the Great Depression came to America.   Many firms went
5 bust and many people lost their jobs.   They lost everything and their children were hungry.

There was no government help for people who lost their jobs, so –
10 when their money ran out – they had to line up for free food. When they could no longer pay their rent, they were put out of their homes.   They had to go to
15 live in 'shanties' – huts made of wood and boxes.

Shanty towns grew up all over America.   They were called **Hoovervilles**, after President
20 Hoover.   Hoover said that the government should not help people who had lost their jobs, or they would get lazy and stop looking for work.

By 1932, few Americans agreed   25
with him.   They elected Franklin D Roosevelt as President.   Roosevelt promised to help the poor and find jobs for the jobless.

Numbers of jobless people in the USA.   In 1933 about a quarter of the workers had no job.

SOURCE Ⓐ

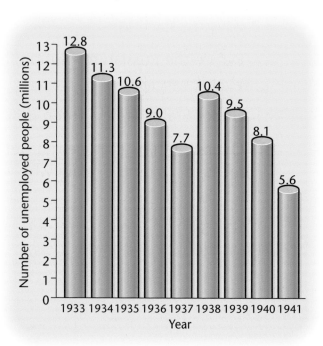

30 **The New Deal**

Roosevelt's plan was called the New Deal. The government set up lots of jobs, eg:

- Building roads and hospitals,

35 - Building dams,

- Planting trees.

This gave jobless people back their pride. It also gave them some money to spend in the

40 shops – which got some of the factories going again.

Roosevelt also gave jobless people $15 a week (about half what you got for a New Deal job). It was

45 not much, and it was only paid for 4 months, but it kept people alive.

The New Deal helped, but it did not end the Depression – that only happened after 1939, when

50 America started making weapons for the Second World War.

Also, the New Deal did not do much to help black Americans. The New Deal jobs were mostly for

55 skilled workers, and few black Americans were skilled workers. Black Americans still did not have equal rights with whites. They said that the government only did

60 something about unemployment when lots of white folk lost their jobs.

SOURCE B

Jobless black people line up for government help.

THINK ABOUT IT

1. Look at Source B. What does it tell us about black Americans during the Depression?

2. Does Source B prove that black people were hurt more than white people by the Depression.

3. Source B says that America had 'the World's Highest Standard of Living'? How was this true?

4. Imagine you are a black American. Write a short speech about the photo in Source B, getting angry about the difference between the poster and the reality of the lives of black Americans.

Use the following words in your speech: *jobless, poor, rights, cheated, change.*

51

The Depression: how did poverty affect people's lives?

SOURCE Ⓐ

Peggy Terry was 10 years old when the Depression started in America.

I knew that something was wrong was when I came home from school.   My mother sent us to go to the soup line.

If you were first in the soup line, all you got was the water on the top, so we asked the man who was putting the soup into our buckets (everyone had to bring their own bucket) to please dip down to get some of the meat and potatoes from the bottom, but he would not do it.

My dad said to us: 'Do you think that life is bad?   Get in the car. I want to show you something.'   And he took us to a Hooverville.

It was a bad place.   There were people living in old rusty cars – I mean that was their home!   There were people living in shacks made of boxes.   One family with a lot of kids was living in a big box.

And this town was 10 miles wide and 15 miles long.

[Peggy married in 1935 when she was 15, and went all over America looking for work.]

One night we walked for a long time, and were so tired and hungry, and a wagon came along.   There was a black family going into town.   They could not eat with the whites, so they cooked their own food.   The back of the wagon was full of hay and they let us sleep there.   When we woke up, they asked us if we wanted to eat with them – they had chicken and potatoes and everything.   It was great.

But I didn't like Black people then.   In fact, I wanted them all to go away.

Remembered by Peggy Terry in the 1960s.

SOURCE Ⓑ

THINK ABOUT IT

Work with a partner to make up an imaginary radio interview with Peggy Terry. Start off by saying something like:

'Peggy Terry is 20 years old. She's been on the road since 1935, with her husband, looking for work.'

Then ask her some questions.

Start off by asking her some questions that 'she' will be able to answer from pages 52–53, e.g.:

- When did you first know something was wrong?
- How did you eat during the Depression?

- Were some people worse off than you?
- Where did jobless people live?
- What did you do to try to find work?
- Did you like black people?

But you can add some other questions which 'Peggy' can answer as the real Peggy might have done, e.g.:

- How did you feel … (about something)?
- Why … (did you do something).
- Do you feel differently about black people now?

A Hooverville in 1940. A family gets ready to cook a meal outside their home.

STOP AND REFLECT:
Think about how the Depression affected Peggy Terry, then write a sentence starting: 'The Depression affected people by …'

The Depression: why did people's experiences differ?

Women in the 1930s

More women got jobs during the Depression than before. A woman did not get as big a wage as a man
5 – in 1937 they only earned half as much. Firms took on more women because they were trying to save money.

So the New Deal did not do much
10 to help women. One New Deal job – building up the banks of rivers to stop them flooding – gave jobs to nearly 3 million people. But only 8,000 of these were
15 women.

SOURCE Ⓐ

An advertisement from 1938 for holiday flights to Hawaii.

SOURCE Ⓑ

David Rossman was a doctor during the 1930s. His patients were rich people. Many years later, Dr Rossman was asked about what was going on during the Depression:

Nothing much. You would not know there was a Depression. Some people did not have a job and they would work for almost nothing.

Your patients were not affected?

Not very much. They still paid their fees. I was making $2,000 a month, which was a lot in those days.

Did you ever meet poor people?

Not much. A builder built me a 10-room stone house for $8,000. I asked him what he got out of it. He said: 'I ate for 6 months!'

An historian called Studs Terkel talked to Dr Rossman.

Businessmen

Businessmen did not like the New Deal. They did not like paying taxes to the government for the wages of the people on the New 20 Deal. They said it was not the job of the government to look after people when they were unemployed or sick.

They said the New Deal should 25 have done more for businessmen.

Support for Roosevelt

The New Deal did not end the Depression – there were still 10
30 million people out of work in 1939. Some people – as we have seen – did not like the New Deal.

Not many people agreed with them.   Most Americans loved
35 Roosevelt.   They knew he was trying to make their lives better. They voted him to be their President FOUR times!

Many years later, people still
40 remembered Roosevelt.   One man said in 1966: 'He was God in this country'.

THINK ABOUT IT

1. **Did the New Deal do much for women?**

2. **Why did businessmen not like the New Deal?**

3. **How do we know that not many Americans agreed with them?**

4. **Look at Sources A and B.   Did the Depression hurt everyone?**

STOP AND REFLECT: Think about the failings of the New Deal, then write a paragraph starting: 'The worst failing of the New Deal was …'

Pulling it Together

Did the New Deal save America from Depression?

It is 1941.   You are a newspaper reporter and you are against the New Deal.   Write a newspaper report to prove that the New Deal is a failure.

FIRST, make up a good headline such as: 'New Deal flops!'

THEN write three paragraphs, in the style of a newspaper article, saying that the New Deal has failed in THREE ways:

- It hasn't done anything for black people.
- It hasn't done anything for women.
- It hasn't ended unemployment.

Make sure you use:

- Strong words such as 'disaster', 'unfair', 'sexist' and 'racist'.
- Personal pronouns such as 'we' and 'you'.

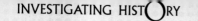

CHAPTER 5

People and War

What was it like to live through 'total war'?

In this chapter you will:

- **Think about the effects of the bombing of Germany.**
- **Study how the government kept people going through the Blitz.**

The Second World War was called a 'total war'. Everybody had to play their part. Some went to fight as soldiers, but at home everybody was affected – e.g. women worked in arms factories,
5 men went to the Home Guard. Many people were bombed and some were killed.

'Bomber' Harris

Towards the end of the war, Britain began to bomb Germany back. Arthur 'Bomber' Harris,
10 the head of the RAF, sent huge bombing raids into Germany. He said that bombing the Germans would make them want to give up, and bombing their factories would stop them supplying their armies (though he knew, in fact,
15 that most bombs missed).

Some people think that he was wrong to bomb Germany like that.

SOURCE Ⓑ

In 1943, American planes bombed a ball-bearing factory. They destroyed it but 60 planes were shot down. The bombing almost wrecked industry in Germany.

Written by a modern historian. The raid cut output of ball bearings (needed for engines) by 67%.

SOURCE Ⓒ

The bombing stopped the Nazis getting oil. It destroyed their roads and railways and wrecked their towns. These were too late to win the war on their own, but they did help to defeat Germany.

Written by a modern historian.

SOURCE Ⓐ

The bombing in Berlin closed all the schools, but less than half the factories stopped – and then only for a short time. The Germans did not want to give up and the bombing failed to stop the factories supplying the army.

Written by a modern historian.

THINK ABOUT IT

1. Why did Britain bomb Germany?
2. The RAF bombed German civilians – were they wrong to do so?
3. Look at Sources A–D. Sort them out into those which say that the bombing was successful, and those which suggest it failed.

Was Bomber Harris right to bomb Germany like that? Think about:
- Did it stop German factories supplying the Nazi army?
- Did it make the Germans want to give up?
- Did it give the British revenge?

Write three paragraphs to argue that Britain was right, or wrong, to bomb Germany.

- Start: 'I think that Britain was (right/ wrong) to bomb Germany … (and explain your argument, using information from the Sources).

- Then write a second paragraph: 'Some people argue against this. They say … But they are wrong because …'

- Then write a final paragraph: 'In conclusion, therefore…'

SOURCE D

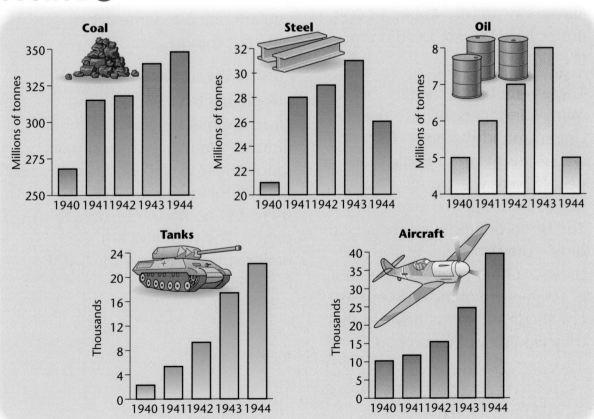

Nazi War Output, 1940–1944 (coal, steel and oil in millions tones).

How do you construct propaganda?

The Blitz

Between September 1940 and May 1941, the Nazi air force (the *Luftwaffe*) bombed Britain. This is
5 called 'the Blitz'. At first the *Luftwaffe* only bombed airfields. But then the British bombed Berlin – so Hitler ordered the Luftwaffe to bomb London.

10 The first *Luftwaffe* attack came when 300 Nazi planes bombed London on 7 September 1940. Then they bombed London every night until the middle of
15 November. After that, they bombed other towns – e.g. Coventry was attacked on 14 November 1940. About 43,000 British people were killed during
20 the Blitz.

There were bomb shelters, but many Londoners went to the Underground stations. They wanted to get in so badly that
25 people were waiting for a place from 10 o'clock in the morning. The Underground was smelly and dirty – they only had buckets for toilets. Other people walked out
30 of town every night and slept in cowsheds and in the fields so that they would not be bombed.

The government was frightened that people would lose heart.

They **censored** the newspapers 35 (kept all the bad things out of the news) and published propaganda to keep people going.

How do you construct propaganda? 40 – using photographs

You MUST work with a partner. You are newspaper reporters during the Blitz – but one of you is British, and the other is a Nazi. You are 45 going to report on the Blitz, but you are going to write very different things!

Editing the photos

It is November 1940 and the 50 Nazis are making many bombing attacks. You have three photos (pages 60–61) of the effects of the bombing. Only ONE of them can go on tomorrow's front 55 page. The Nazi and British newspapers will show the SAME PICTURE!!!

THINK ABOUT IT

Study the pictures on pages 60–61.

1. Working with your partner and using the grid below, think about how you could use the photos in Sources A–C. Remember that the British reporter will want to use them in a very different way to the Nazi!

   Choose one photo.

2. a) The 'British reporter' writes a caption of 20-or-so words about the photo you have chosen. Remember that it must be morale-boosting and positive – it must make the British readers want to carry on with the war.

   b) The 'Nazi reporter' writes a caption of 20-or-so words about the photo you have chosen. Remember that it must be morale-boosting FOR THE NAZIS – it must make the Nazi readers think that the war is going well.

3. Compare your caption with your partner's – which is the better propaganda? Explain your answer.

4. Finally, write a paragraph to explain why the two accounts are so different.

Photo	What the British reporter would say it showed	What the Nazi reporter would say it showed
A: Pulling a person out of a bombed house.		
B: Londoners sleeping in an Underground station		The British are so frightened of our bombs that they are living like rats underground.
C: The King and Queen see how Buckingham Palace has been bombed.	The King and Queen have been bombed too – but they too are not downhearted. We are all in this together, and together we shall win!	

Background to the photos

Photo A: 1.5 million British people gave up their spare time every night during the bombing. They worked as rescue workers, plane spotters or firemen; some just made cups of tea.   It was dangerous working in bombed buildings.

Photo B: At first, the government said that people could NOT use the Underground as shelters, but people were so afraid that the government was forced to let them.

The Underground was not totally safe – sometimes bombs got through and killed people there.

Photo C: On 13 September, 1940, Nazi bombs fell on some of the buildings at Buckingham Palace (not the Palace itself).   At first, the news was censored, but then the event was made public. The King and Queen were pleased that they had been bombed because it showed that they were in danger like everyone else.   'Now I can look the Londoners in the face', said the Queen.

PHOTO Ⓐ

Workers bring out a person from a bombed house.

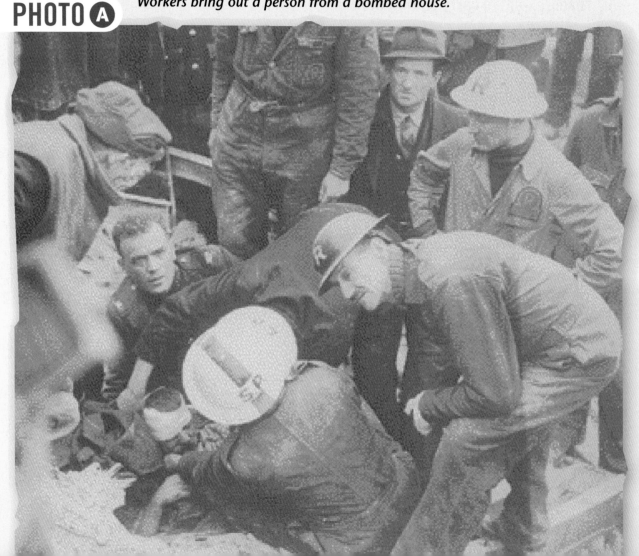

PHOTO B

Londoners sleeping in an Underground station.

PHOTO C

The King and Queen see how Buckingham Palace has been bombed.

61

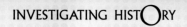

How do you construct propaganda? – using written sources

Now you are going to do for written sources what you did for the photographs on pages 60–61. First, you will study Sources A–D on this page and choose which source you are going to use, then you will write stories based on the source you have chosen.

SOURCE A

After one attack on Bristol, Churchill went to see the people. This is what an American wrote about his visit:

People were cooking in half-bombed houses. Churchill went to see the places that had been hit worst. He walked through the streets on his own.

The people rushed over to him. They shouted: 'Good old Churchill – you will never let us down'.

People had just been bombed. No one had got any sleep that night. But two hours after Churchill had been there, the town was back on its feet.

SOURCE B

This is what one man wrote on 17 September 1940.

The people in London are very angry. The King and Queen were booed when they went to see some bombed houses the other day. The Government is very worried about this.

SOURCE C

This is a newspaper report from 1940 about the men who worked in the railway stations.

The stations were hit and the trains smashed up. But even while the bombs were falling, the railwaymen were out, working in the dark to try to mend the railways lines. They worked all night, and many of them were hurt by the bombs, but they got the job done.

SOURCE D

This is what an American newspaperman wrote about London:

We went to see a place where the church and houses had been bombed. There were lots of people. One woman with a baby said to me: 'It will take a million bombs to beat us.'

Everywhere is smashed up. But everyone has found a new spirit. 6 million brave people are standing up to Hitler, so that they can save the world from evil.

Source	What the British reporter will like about this story.	What the Nazi reporter will like about this story.
A	People keeping going. Everyone loved Churchill …	Lots of houses hit …
B		
C	Railway workers brave and work all night …	
D		

THINK ABOUT IT

Pretend to be a British, or a Nazi, reporter. Choose a Source on page 62, and use the table above to work out which facts you are going to concentrate on. Now write a 'newspaper story' about the event in a way which will encourage the people of your own country.

STOP AND REFLECT: Write a paragraph about what you have learned about propaganda during the war.

Pulling it Together

What was it like to live through 'total war'?

Look back over the last chapter and make a list of phrases describing what life was like for Londoners during the Blitz (clue words: *Luftwaffe*, Blitz, Underground, sleeping in the fields, propaganda, Buckingham Palace, firemen, rescue workers, Churchill, railways, spirit).

Write:

1. An information passage for a children's encyclopaedia on 'Life on the Home Front'. Remember to start with a general statement, and to write your account under a series of sub-headings. Use impersonal language, and avoid emotive words – concentrate on the facts and figures.

2. A letter to a friend about the bombing raids. Here you will not need to write in logical order, but express your personal feelings and opinions, and use lots of powerful verbs adjectives and adverbs.

CHAPTER 6

The Jewish Tragedy
How did the war change Nazi treatment of the Jews?

In this chapter you will:

- Learn how the Nazis treated the Jews during the war.
- Find out what the 'Final Solution' was.
- Study what life was like in a death camp.
- Think about why the Holocaust happened.

'The Jewish Question'

Hitler had always hated the Jews. Jews in Germany were picked on and bullied from the time Hitler
5 came to power in 1933.

But when the Nazis went into Poland, they found 3 million Jews living there. Thy did not know what to do with them, so they
10 made them all go and live together in the poorest houses in towns – in places called '**ghettos**'. These places were so bad that more than half a million Jews in
15 Poland died, 1939–1941.

Some Nazis said that the Jews should be made to work as slaves. Some said that they should be left in the ghettos. They called this
20 their 'Jewish problem'.

Jewish men, women and children stand by a grave, waiting to be shot. One child takes a last look behind her.

SOURCE Ⓐ

And then Hitler invaded Russia. Suddenly, the Nazis were faced with a
25 war which they were NOT winning easily, and with 5 million Russian Jews. Hitler had always said that
30 the Germans were in a 'life or death' war with the Jews and the Communists. Now that seemed to be
35 coming true. So the Nazis tried to kill all the Jews in Russia.

At first, the Nazis tried to kill the Jews
40 by shooting them (see Source B).

SOURCE B

They did not weep or cry. They stood together in families, hugging and saying goodbye. One old grandma sang to a little child and tickled it – the child was happy. The mother and father looked on, tears in their eyes. The father held his 10-year-old boy by the hand. The boy was trying not to cry. The father pointed to the sky – he seemed to be telling the boy something. A girl walked past me – she said: 'Twenty-three!'

I went to look at the grave. There were already about 1,000 bodies in it. I looked to see who was killing them. A Nazi soldier sat on the edge of the grave, his legs swinging over the side. He had a gun and smoked a cigarette.

The people were made to take their clothes off, and then they climbed into the grave onto the bodies of those who had been shot. They lay down on top of them. Then I heard the sound of guns shooting. I looked into the pit and saw the bodies moving, or the heads sinking down onto the bodies below, blood coming from their necks.

I am saying this in Germany on 10 November 1945. I swear to God that it is true.

An eye-witness story by a young German, Hermann Graebe, of how the Nazis shot Jews in Russia in 1942.

THINK ABOUT IT

1. Read Source B. Graebe wrote without using any words which showed that he was sad, or horrified or angry – the passage shows no feelings. Re-write it (or part of it) using words which make clear that you are upset, horrified and angry.

2. Graebe was not a soldier. He noted the killings in his diary, but did nothing to try to stop them. Is he as much to blame for the killings as the Nazi soldier he saw doing the shooting?

What was the final solution?

The Wannsee Conference, 1942

In Bible times, the Jews used to burn an animal as an offering to God – they called this a 'holocaust'.

5 Nowadays, we use the word 'holocaust' for the mass-killings of Jewish people by the Nazis.

Shooting was slow and messy. So, in January 1942 the Nazi leaders
10 met at Wannsee, just outside Berlin in Germany. The Nazis had conquered all of mainland Europe. It looked as if they were going to win the war. They knew that they
15 wanted to kill all the Jews in Europe. So, now, they sat down and worked out a plan.

Today, we cannot understand the minds of men who sat round and
20 calmly talked about murdering a whole race of people. But the Nazis thought that it was a good idea. They called their idea: 'The **Final Solution**'.

25 Death factories

The Nazis built death camps. The Jews arrived by rail. Within 2 hours of arriving they were gassed.

The Jews were tricked. They were
30 told that they had to go for a shower. If the Jews panicked or tried to fight, the camp would not run on time.

SOURCE Ⓐ

When we open the doors, they are all dead. They are all standing up pressed together in the chambers. You can tell which are the families – they are all holding hands.

The bodies are so close together that you have to tear them apart from each other. The gassed Jews have wet and messed themselves, and they are covered in blood.

The workers throw out the bodies of the children. They have to work fast. Men open the mouths looking for gold teeth.

Written in 1945 by an SS soldier who saw Jews gassed at a death camp in 1942.

The mathematics of murder

The people who were to be 35 gassed were pushed into a big gas chamber. At Auschwitz in Poland – one of the biggest death camps – there were 4 gas chambers, and 6,000 people could fit into each. 40

The Nazis dropped pellets of poison gas – called Zyklon B – into the chamber through a grill at the top. It took 10 minutes for the people to die. Then the doors 45 were opened and a team of Jewish prisoners was sent in to pull out the bodies and take them to be burned.

SOURCE B

This drawing of Jews going to the gas chamber was made by David Olere. The Nazis let him live because he drew pictures for them. They made him work in the gas chambers taking out the bodies.

THINK ABOUT IT

1. Why do you think the Nazis called the plan to gas all the Jews 'the Final Solution'.

2. Why did the Nazis tell the Jews they were going for a shower?

3. The SS soldier who wrote Source A shot himself. Why do you think he did this?

4. The Nazis never said they killed the Jews. They used words like 'processed' and 'special treatment'. Why do you think they did this?

STOP AND REFLECT:
Write a paragraph starting: 'In their 'Final Solution', the Nazis ...'

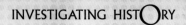

What was life like in the death camps?

The selection

Camps like Auschwitz had two jobs.

First, they were places to mass-murder the Jews. But they were also work-camps.

5 When a new set of Jews came to the camp, people who were over 15, and well and strong, were picked out.   They were called 'work-Jews'.

Everyone else – the old, the sick, and women with children – was sent straight to the gas
10 chambers.

The 'work-Jews' lived for about 3 months.   They got almost no food and were made to work like slaves.   Many of them fell ill and died.

Every time a new set of Jews came to the camp,
15 the Nazis took all the 'work-Jews' who were sick or weak, and sent them to the gas chambers.

SOURCE B

One woman always used to carry her bit of bread with her, so that she would not die of hunger.

One day, she dropped it into the toilet pit.   So she jumped into the pit, to get her bit of bread.   She, and the bread, were filthy, but she did not care.

Like an animal, all she wanted was to have food … to stay alive.

Written in 1985 by a Jewish woman who had been in a death camp when she was a 13-year-old girl during the war.

SOURCE A

Here is a woman – she walks quickly and seems calm.   A small child with a round, pretty face runs after her.   He holds out his arms and says: 'Mama!   Mama!'

'Pick up your child,' the soldier says.

'It is not mine, not mine!' she screams, and she hides her face in her hands.   She wants to go with the work-Jews …   She wants to live.

A Polish prisoner tells what one woman did when she saw that women with children were being sent to be gassed.
This was written in a book by T. Borowski.   Borowski was not a Jew, so the Nazis let him live if he helped them kill the Jews.   He felt so bad about what he had done that, in 1951, he killed himself.

SOURCE C

This is a drawing made by a Polish prisoner at Auschwitz, 1943–1945.

Food

A 'work-Jew' was supposed to get
350 grams of bread for breakfast,
20 and 1 litre of potato soup for lunch
and evening meal.   Four times a
week, they were supposed to get
20 grams of meat.   But they never
got anything like as much as this.

25 Some 'work-Jews' threw
themselves alive into the fires
rather than go on doing what the
Nazis told them.   But some people
wanted to live.

30 If you wanted to live, you had to
be cunning.   It was no good
rushing to the front to be first to
get the soup.   The soup at the top
was thin and watery. Better wait
35 to the end, and get some of the
potatoes at the bottom!

If you wanted to live, you had to
do anything and eat anything.

THINK ABOUT IT

1. Why did so many work-Jews die from disease in the camps?
2. Why did the woman in Source A pretend the child wasn't her son?
3. Why is this so shocking?
4. What do Sources A, B and C tell us about life in the camps?
5. Borowski (Source A) helped the Nazis.   Should he have been put on trial for war crimes?
6. Nazis who took part in killing the Jews are still being discovered – but they are very old now.   Do you think it is too late to put them on trial for war crimes?

STOP AND REFLECT: Look back at Sources A, B and C. Think about which Source is the most shocking, then write a paragraph starting: 'Source [???] shocked me most because …'

What were conditions like in the death camps?

Dying conditions

Not just Jews lived in the camps – there were other people the Nazis hated, such as Communists and homosexuals – but the Jews
5 had the worst life and food.   Men and women lived in different huts.   Everyone had a uniform (which soon became a dirty rag), a plate and a pair of clogs.

SOURCE A

Every morning the prisoners had to   10 stand outside.   The **SS** soldiers called out their names to see if anyone had died. Any prisoners who   15 had broken the rules were punished, in public.   If it was very cold, some prisoners died during the   20 roll-call.

The prisoners slept on bunks.   The bunks were just planks of wood with gaps in   25 between.   There was no bedding.   If you had a lower bunk, and the person above you was ill,   30 mess dropped down onto you through the gaps.

Inside a gas chamber by David Olere.

SOURCE B

The three prisoners stood on the chairs. Three ropes were put round their necks.

'Long live freedom!' shouted the two men. The child did not say anything. 'Where is God?' said a man behind me. Then the chairs were kicked over.

We were made to walk past and look at them. The two men were dead. Their blue, swollen tongues were hanging out.

But the child was not heavy enough, so the third rope was still moving. The child was still alive.

For more than half an hour he hung there, dying in agony before our eyes. Behind me, the man said again: 'Where is God now?'

Inside me, a voice said: 'He is here – He is hanging here dying'.

That night, the soup tasted of corpses.

Written in 1982 by a Jewish man who had been in a death camp when he was a 15-year-old boy during the war.

SOURCE C

Often, they used to cut the skin off the dead prisoners. It was left in the sun to dry. Then it was made into things like gloves, slippers and handbags. Everyone wanted something made of skin that had a tattoo!

Also, we often got asked for skulls or bones – so we would have to boil the bodies. The SS soldiers like to get ones with good teeth.

Written by Dr Franz Blaha, who also used the death camp prisoners for medical experiments.

THINK ABOUT IT

1. Read Source B. Does it show that the Jewish prisoners lost their faith in God?

2. What effects might a public execution have had on the Jewish prisoners? Think about:
   - The horror of watching it.
   - The fear of it happening to them.
   - The way they would have behaved afterwards.

STOP AND REFLECT: Think about how the Nazis used cruelty to break the prisoners' spirit, then write a paragraph starting: 'Life in the camps affected the prisoners' spirit ...'

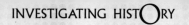

Pulling it Together

How did the war change Nazi treatment of the Jews?

Some Germans had always hated the Jews, but it was the Second World War which led them to try to kill all the Jews in Europe. Scan pages 28–31 and 64–71 to remind yourself how the Nazis treated the Jews. Then study pages 72–73.

Writing the Essay

- In the first paragraph, copy 'Some Germans had always hated the Jews', then explain how this helped Hitler.

- In the second paragraph, copy 'Nazi propaganda encouraged Germans to hate the Jews', then explain how this helped Hitler.

- In the third paragraph, copy 'In the Second World War, Hitler conquered Russia and Poland' then explain how this led to the 'Final Solution'.

- Finally, copy 'The Nazis set up Death Camps', and write a long paragraph using pages 66–71 to describe how the Nazis went about killing the Jews.

A. Some Germans had always hated the Jews.

Martin Luther was a German monk in the 16th century. This is what he wrote in 1543.

The Jews are robbers and everything they eat and everything they have has been stolen from us. That is how they live – by stealing things from us. We work, but they get rich – we stay poor because of them. What should we Christians do with these bad people, the Jews?

We should set fire to everything they have, and destroy their houses.

Written by Martin Luther.

D. The Nazis set up death camps.

B. Hitler encouraged Germans to hate the Jews.

How did cruel treatment turn into mass murder?

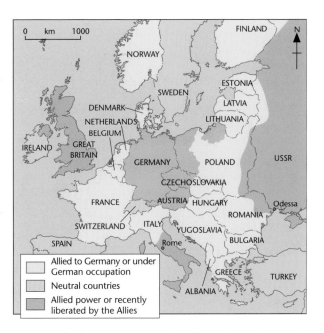

C. Hitler conquered Poland and Russia,
where there were many Jews.

CHAPTER 7

The World Divided

Why was there a Cold War after the Second World War?

In this chapter you will:

- Learn why there was a 'Cold War' after the Second World War.
- Find out how a young man was killed trying to cross the Berlin Wall.
- Study the Cuban Missiles crisis.
- Learn how the Cold War ended.

Why did a 'Cold War' start?

SOURCE A *The differences between Communism and Capitalism.*

Living standards are low but everyone has a job and there is less of a difference between rich and poor.

Living standards are much higher but there is a bigger difference between rich and poor people.

During the Second World War, Britain, America and Russia fought together against Hitler. But they hated each other. This hatred

5 went right back to 1917, when Russia became a Communist country – Britain and America sent armies to try to destroy the Communists (see Chapter 3).

10 Even by 1945, little had changed. Britain and America thought that Russia wanted to spread Communism all over the world. The Russians feared that America

15 would use the atomic bomb to destroy them. The two sides dare not fight each other – no one dared to have an atomic war. So they had a war without fighting –

20 called the 'Cold War' – instead.

Europe after 1945

After the Second World War, many eastern European countries were left under Russian control.

Britain and America wanted them 25 to become free countries. But Stalin kept control of a ring of countries round Russia – in case Germany ever attacked again. People in these countries who did 30 NOT want Communism were killed. Western democracy and freedom were not wanted.

In 1946, Winston Churchill, the British Prime Minister, said that an 35 '**Iron Curtain**' had come down between the democratic countries of the west and the Communist countries of the east.

SOURCE Ⓑ *Map of Europe in 1949.*

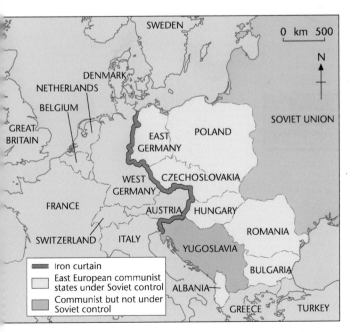

Iron curtain

East European communist states under Soviet control

Communist but not under Soviet control

THINK ABOUT IT

Looking at the map of Europe in 1949, what about it would please Stalin, the ruler of Russia?

STOP AND REFLECT: Read pages 74–75 and discuss with a friend who you think was to blame for starting the Cold War. Write a paragraph starting:
'I blame [...] most for starting the Cold War because ...'

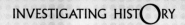

How did the Cold War get colder?

Divided Germany

After the war, Russia, America, Britain and France split Germany into four 'zones'. Russia turned its
5 zone into a Communist country cut off from the West by the Iron Curtain.

Berlin was also split into four zones, but it was deep inside the Russian
10 zone. So the Americans, British and French zones of Berlin were a free land of democracy *behind* the Iron Curtain. Stalin did NOT like this! In 1948 he shut off all road and rail transport into Berlin – he 15 wanted to starve Berlin so he could take it over and make it part of the Russian zone.

The Americans did not want to go to war. Instead – for 13 months – 20 they flew into Berlin everything the Berliners needed to live (the 'Berlin Airlift').

In the end, Stalin had to give up. He dare not go to war – the 25 Americans had the atomic bomb and he did not.

SOURCE Ⓐ

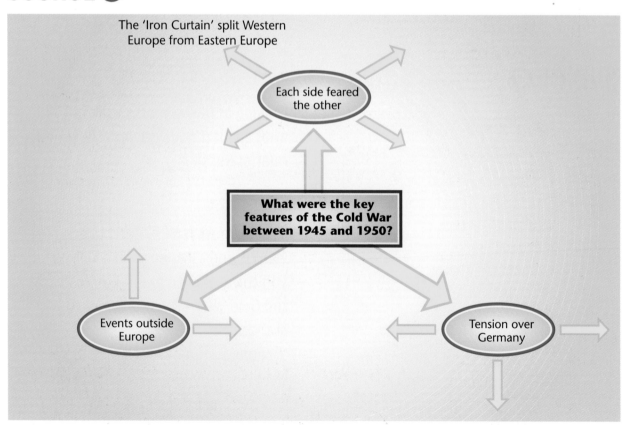

Aspects of the Cold War.

The Cold War goes global

30 In 1949, however, Russia got the atomic bomb. That same year, China turned Communist. The

35 whole world seemed to be turning Communist.

In 1950, in the far east, the Communist

40 state of North Korea invaded the democratic country of South Korea. America sent

45 400,000 soldiers to help South Korea. After 3 years of war, the fighting stopped – South Korea was

50 still a free country.

In the 1960s, the Communist state of North Vietnam tried to conquer the

55 democratic country of South Vietnam. Again, America sent soldiers to help – but this time it was a

60 disaster. In 1973 the Americans had to pull out of Vietnam, and in 1975, South Vietnam fell to the

65 Communists.

THINK ABOUT IT

1. Source A suggests that there were three 'Aspects of the Cold War'. Working with a friend, split the 9 'Events of the Cold War' (below) into the three categories in Source A. (One has been done for you already.)

2. Imagine you have to write about 'The Cold War' for an encyclopaedia. Write your entry in three sections:
   a) Each side feared the other
   b) Tension over Germany
   c) Events outside Europe.

Events of the Cold War

1 1945: America dropped the first atomic bomb.

2 Berlin and Germany were split between the West and Russia.

3 *The 'Iron Curtain' split Western Europe from Eastern Europe.*

4 Russia took control of Eastern Europe.

5 1948–1949: Stalin cut off West Berlin.

6 1948–1949: Berlin Airlift.

7 1949: Russia got the atomic bomb.

8 1949: the Communists took power in China.

9 1950–1953: Korean War.

STOP AND REFLECT: Scan pages 74–77 and discuss with a friend why America and Russia so feared and hated each other. Write a paragraph starting: 'America and Russia hated each other because ...'

Why was the 'Wall' such a deadly place?

Germany was still a big problem in the 1950s. Berlin had not fallen to Russia in 1949, and it was still a big worry to the Communists.

5 The West was much richer than Communist eastern Europe, and life was better there. The people of the Communist east were cut off from Western Europe by the
10 Iron Curtain, but – in Berlin – they could just walk into West Berlin and fly to America. Millions left – most of them young and skilled. East Germany was losing all its
15 best people.

So, in 1961, the East German government built a wall across the city. It split Berlin in two. People living in East Berlin could not visit their families in West Berlin. 20

Anybody who tried to escape to West Germany over the wall was shot.

About 100 East Berliners lost their lives trying to cross the Wall. 25

SOURCE A

Peter Fechter was an 18-year-old bricklayer from East Berlin. He wanted to live in West Berlin, where his sister lived. The only problem was the Wall, which stood between him and her. With a friend, he made a plan to get out, using an empty building near to the Wall.

On 15 August 1962, they checked out the building. It had a window near the Wall. They knew what they were doing was dangerous. In the last year, 49 East Berliners had died trying to get over the Wall.

On 17 August they went into the building. They climbed through the window, dropped to the ground, and then ran across the open space to the Wall. Helmut got to the Wall and climbed over. Just as he dropped down to the other side and freedom, he saw Peter.

Peter was not climbing. He was scared.

Then the shooting began. Peter tried to climb the Wall but he was hit in the back .

He fell back. He was bleeding badly. He was calling for help.

The West Berliners saw what was happening. They asked the East German soldiers to help Peter, but they did nothing – they were still pointing their guns at Peter. They asked the American soldiers on the West side to go and help, but they said: 'This is not our problem.'

After 50 minutes, the East German soldiers went to get Peter's body. He had bled to death.

www.swlink.net

SOURCE ⑧

Peter's body next to the Wall – on the East German side.

THINK ABOUT IT

The story in Source A is a recount text. It tells the story of what Peter did and how he died.

Now you have to rewrite the story as a persuasion text. Start by going through the story with a friend, making a list of all the things that Americans would think were terrible and bad.

Imagine that you are writing about this event for an American newspaper, to show the readers just how terrible the Wall is. Remember to use words like: 'brave', 'desperate', heartless', 'evil', 'murder' and 'tragedy'.

What are you NOT going to mention?

STOP AND REFLECT: Scan back over pages 75–79, then write paragraphs starting:

'The Communists built the Wall because ...'

'The Wall made the West hate the Communists more because ...'

Why did the 'Cuban missiles crisis' occur?

SOURCE Ⓐ

This Russian ship seems to be carrying Russian bomber planes in 'kit' form to Cuba. These planes could bomb places 2,400 km (1,500 miles) away.

The Bay of Pigs incident

In 1959, Fidel Castro (a Communist) took power in Cuba. The Americans were not happy –
5 Cuba was only 150 km (90 miles) away from America! In 1961 the Americans gave guns to some Cubans who hated Castro, and helped them try to invade Cuba, at
10 a place called 'the Bay of Pigs'.

The attack was a total flop. But the Bay of Pigs had one result. Castro asked the Russians to help him. So, in 1962, the Russians set
15 up **nuclear missiles** in Cuba.

The Americans were frightened. They had to get rid of the missiles, whatever the cost. The world was on the brink of nuclear war – until
20 Russia agreed to take back the missiles.

THINK ABOUT IT

You work for the American government. You have just been given Sources A, B and C. Your job is to write a report for the President. The chart opposite tells you what you need to know to write it:

In your report:
● Tell the President what the Sources show is happening in Cuba.
● Assess how much danger there is to America.
● Choose the best thing he could do (and explain why).

SOURCE B

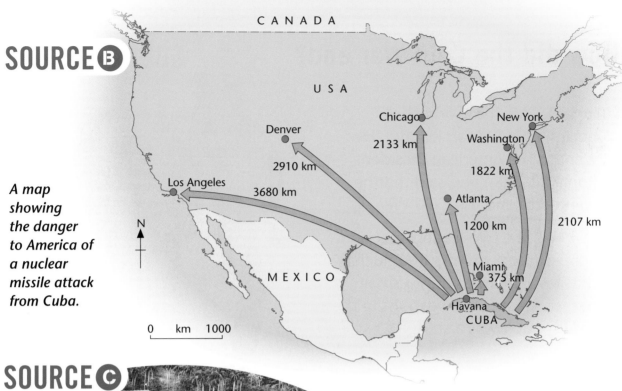

A map showing the danger to America of a nuclear missile attack from Cuba.

CANADA

USA

Chicago

2133 km

New York

Washington

1822 km

Denver

2910 km

Los Angeles

3680 km

Atlanta

1200 km

2107 km

N

MEXICO

Miami

375 km

Havana

CUBA

0   km   1000

SOURCE C

LAUNCH POSITION

MISSILE-READY TENTS

MISSILE ERECTORS

A photo of a Russian missile base in Cuba, taken by an American plane.

STOP AND REFLECT:
Write a paragraph starting: 'In 1962 the world was on the brink of war because ...'

Source	What does it show?	How bad is it?	What might we do about it?
A	This Russian ship seems to be carrying Russian bomber planes in 'kit' form to Cuba.	These planes could bomb many places in America, but they cannot carry nuclear missiles.	We could: • Sink the Russian ships • Tell the Russians to turn back • Stop the ships from reaching Cuba.
B	A map showing the danger of a nuclear missile base.	The nuclear missiles could get to any place in America.	We could: • Bomb the missile sites • Threaten war if Russia does not take away the missiles • Wait to see if the Russian ships turn back.
C	A photo of a Russian missile base in Cuba.	The sites will be ready to fire missiles in a few days.	

How did the Cold War end?

In 1985, Mikhail Gorbachev
became the Russian leader.   He
went to the American President
Ronald Reagan and said that he
5   wanted to end the Cold War.

In 1987, the two leaders met and
agreed to get rid of 3,800 nuclear
missiles.   This was only a small
part of the nuclear weapons in the
10   world, but it was a start.

The end of Communism

By 1985, Russia was in trouble.
Gorbachev wanted to cut the
number of nuclear weapons
15   because Russia could no longer
afford to make them.

Gorbachev knew that he had to
modernise Russia.   He began to
make changes.   He stopped
20   bullying the countries of eastern
Europe.   But he found he had
started something he could not
stop.   One by one, the countries
of eastern Europe threw out their
25   Communist governments.

In 1991, some Communist army
leaders in Russia arrested
Gorbachev.   They tried to stop the
changes he was making.   But they
30   failed – the people did not want
Communism.   By the end of 1991,
Communism had ended in Russia.

SOURCE Ⓐ

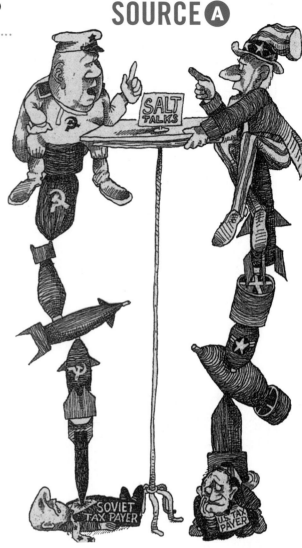

An American cartoon of 1970.   Russia and American were talking about the need to cut the number of nuclear weapons.

SOURCE Ⓑ

The Russian government said that HALF its money was spent on nuclear weapons and the army.   To pay for them, the Russian people had to go without things.

America spent only 10% of its money on weapons in the 1960s, and only 6% in the 1980s.

Written by a modern historian.

SOURCE C

In the winter of 1990–1991, the Russians went short of everything. Next winter, things were worse. One week, there was no milk. If there was milk, there was no meat. For a while there were no tomatoes, no shoes. If there was fruit, there was no toilet paper. Factories closed because they had no heating.

Communism had turned out to be a disaster. Russian industry was no good. Everything was always sold at a loss. Bread cost 20 kopeks to buy, but 60 kopeks to make.

Written by a modern historian.

THINK ABOUT IT

1. Look at Source A. Does it want America and Russia to be friends?

2. Why was 1987 a turning point in the Cold War?

3. How does Source B explain WHY Russia wanted to end the Cold War?

4. What does Source C tell us about life in Communist Russia?

Pulling it Together

Why was there a cold war after the Second World War?

Interviewing Gorbachev in 1992

The Cold War is over. So now is the time when historians begin to think about it – why it happened, how dangerous it really was, and why it came to an end.

Imagine that you are interviewing Mikhail Gorbachev. Work in pairs. One of you pretend to be an historian; get your friend to 'be' Gorbachev. Devise an interview to perform in front of the class.

Here are some of the questions you might ask:

- Who was to blame for starting the Cold War in 1945?
- Why did Russia try to take over all of eastern Europe?
- Was Stalin wrong to try to take over Berlin in 1948?
- Surely you agree that the Berlin Wall of 1961 was wrong?
- How close did we come to nuclear war in 1962?
- Why did you bring the Cold War to an end after 1985?
- Do you regret that Communism has collapsed in eastern Europe?

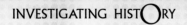

CHAPTER 8

Complex Conflicts

What has been the role of religion, politics, and money in causing recent conflicts?

In this chapter you will:

- **Find out why Yugoslavia fell apart.**
- **Think about why the World Trade Center was attacked in 2001.**
- **Discuss the reasons for conflict in the modern world.**

When you hear about religion causing wars, you tend to think that we must be talking about times long ago.   You may have 5 studied how religion declined in Britain in the 19th century, and, nowadays, religion tends to play a very small part in many British people's lives.

10 But, in fact, religion has played a very important part in the wars of the 20th century – most of all after 1945!!

When India got independence in 15 1947, Hindus, Muslims and Sikhs fought and killed each other. Today, both Hindu India and Muslim Pakistan have the atomic bomb, and in 2001 they came 20 close to a nuclear war.

In Northern Ireland, there has been fighting between the Protestants and the Catholics – more than 3,000 people have been killed since 1969. 25

In the Middle East, the Jewish state of Israel has had wars with the Muslim Arab states nearby.

Very often, there are other things at stake.   In Northern Ireland, 30 some Catholics want to be part of Southern Ireland, and in the Middle East, the problem is oil. But religion is still vital in world politics at the start of the 21st 35 century.

SOURCE Ⓐ

Map showing how Yugoslavia fell apart in the early 1990s.

What was the Bosnian nightmare?

In 1995 – 50 years after the end of the Second World War – there was a war in Europe again. People went to war over Yugoslavia.

5 Yugoslavia had been created by the Treaty of Versailles in 1919. The makers of the Treaty believed that people of the same race had the right to be ruled by their own

10 government, so it set up a country for the southern (*yugo-*) Slavs of Europe. After 1945, Yugoslavia became a Communist country, with a strong ruler called Tito.

The problem was that in 15
Yugoslavia there was not just one race, but there were six. After Tito died in 1980, Yugoslavia began to fall apart. What made it worse was that the different races had 20 different religions.

The worst trouble was in a part of Yugoslavia called Bosnia. Here, the Muslim Bosnians and the Christian Serbs clashed. 25

In 1992, civil war broke out in Bosnia – and 200,000 people were killed in the war.

The Bosnian Serbs –
30 helped by the Serbs in
nearby Serbia – had
the better weapons,
and they began to
win the war.

35 Wherever they took
over, they mass-killed
the Muslims and
drove them out of the
area.

40 In 1994, the two sides
agreed to stop
fighting, but the
Serbs kept on
attacking and driving
45 out the Muslims. It
was the worst mass-
killing in Europe since
Hitler's holocaust.

So, in 1995, the rest
50 of the world stepped
in. Led by America,
they bombed the
Serbs until they
stopped.

STOP AND REFLECT:
Scan back over pages
85–86, then write a
paragraph starting:
'There was war in
Bosnia in 1992–1995
because ...'

THINK ABOUT IT

1. When Yugoslavia fell apart, why did Bosnia cause the biggest problem?
2. Why, do you think, did Yugoslavia not fall apart when Tito was alive?
3. Why did the Bosnian Serbs win the civil war at first?
4. The world let Hitler mass-murder the Jews from 1940 until 1945. In 1995, they stepped in quickly to stop the Serbs in Bosnia. Explain the difference.
5. When some Serbs were put on trial for the mass-killings, they said they were only soldiers obeying orders. Is this an acceptable excuse?

SOURCE B

A Muslim soldier prays by the grave of his friend in Bosnia in 1994.

86

Why were people used as bombs at Novi Travnik?

THINK ABOUT IT

1. Anthony Loyd, who wrote Source A, was a news reporter. From the way he writes, do you think he supports one side or the other? Think about:
   - Why he wrote the story.
   - The way he wrote the story.
   - How the story makes the reader feel about the Muslims.

2. 'The enemy' in the story was not the Serbs, but another race – the Croats. What does this tell you about the war in Bosnia?

SOURCE A

This story comes from 1993. The town of Novi Travnik is in Bosnia.

'Don't shoot! Don't shoot!'

Three soldiers walked up the hill in the rain towards the Muslim soldiers defending Novi Travnik.

A few days ago, they had been captured by the enemy. Now, the enemy was making them go back. With bombs strapped to their chests. Behind them was a thin wire, running back to the enemy lines. The human bombs were coming home.

At they got close, the Muslim leader told his men to shoot them. The soldiers refused. The men were from Novi Travnik. They were their friends. The Muslim soldiers were shouting at each other. The three men kept on walking. The Muslim soldiers fell back.

When the three men got to the Muslim trench there were three bangs, so close together that they made one loud roar. Blood, flesh and metal flew through the air.

For a while, nothing happened. A few soldiers peeped over the top of the trench. All they could see were three pairs of legs. That was all that was left of their friends.

Told by a British newspaperman who saw the war in Bosnia.

STOP AND REFLECT: Write a paragraph starting: 'The war in Bosnia was so nasty because …'

Why did Admira and Bosko die?

Admira and Bosko: the facts

- Bosko and Admira were boyfriend and girlfriend. They were both 25. They had been
5 together for 9 years.

- He was a Christian Serb and she was a Muslim. Mixed friendships like that were common before the war.

10 - When the trouble started in 1992, Admira's mother was asked whether the war would stop their love: 'Only a bullet would end their love for each
15 other', she said.

- In 1993, the Serb army attacked the town. Life was dangerous. In May 1993, Bosko and Admira decided to try to get out.

20 - The only way out was across a bridge, which was VERY dangerous. They might get shot.

- Admira spoke to her friends in the Muslim army; she made them promise not to shoot 25 them.

- Together, the two young people ran across the bridge. They had almost made it to the other side when a bullet hit 30 Bosko. He fell down dead. A second bullet hit Admira. She dragged herself over to Bosko's body and put her arms around him until she, too, died. 35

- No one dared to go out onto the bridge to get the bodies, for fear of getting shot. So it was 8 days before their bodies were buried. 40

The bodies of Bosko and Admira on the bridge, May 1993. Three years later they were re-buried, in a Muslim graveyard.

SOURCE Ⓐ

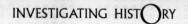

SOURCE B

Front-page outline.

Newspaper Date

NEWSPAPER TITLE

LEAD STORY HEADLINE

Interview with one of the friends of Bosko or Admira

Possible questions:

How do young people feel about this war?

Do you think that couples with different religions can ever be happy together in Bosnia?

Do you see any way of ending this war?

Write your caption here

BACKGROUND TO THE CRISIS IN BOSNIA: HOW DID IT ALL START?

THINK ABOUT IT

The sad story of Bosko and Admira was reported in the newspapers in May 1993.

There are two kinds of newspaper. 'Broadsheets' (such as *The Times*) concentrate on explanation and facts.

'Tabloids' (such as *The Sun*) concentrate more on the 'human interest' and use easy words.

Your task is to write a tabloid newspaper front-page story about Bosko and Admira, using the facts listed on page 88.

1. Make up an attention-grabbing headline.

2. Write the story, trying to make the readers feel sad for the young couple – use words like 'love', 'innocent', 'heartbroken', and 'tragic'. Concentrate on their love and death.

3. Talk about who is to BLAME for the tragedy.

What is the 'New Terrorism'?

5

much terror that the people let them have what they want.

10 There have been many terrorist groups in the past.   An example in Britain is the IRA.

Osama bin Laden

In the 1990s, a new terrorism came
15 about.   It was started by a small group led by Osama bin Laden.

Osama bin Laden came from a very rich Muslim family, but in the 1980s he gave it all up.   In 1979,
20 the Russians had invaded Afghanistan.   Bin Laden set up a group called *al-Qaeda* (meaning 'the Base') to try and drive them out.

25 The Americans wanted the Russians out of Afghanistan too, so they gave Afghan fighters weapons and money.   But, when the Russians had been defeated, bin
30 Laden turned to attack the United States – who he saw as the REAL enemy.

Bin Laden believed that the American way of life is evil – that it is making the rest of the world 35 poor.   He wanted to drive the Americans out of the Middle East.

America needs oil from the Middle East, and has had close links with countries like Saudi Arabia.   Bin 40 Laden wanted to overthrow the rulers of Saudi Arabia and turn it into what he calls a 'true' Muslim country.

Why terrorism? 45

Bin Laden and *al-Qaeda* knew that they could not defeat the Americans in a war.   That is why they used terrorism.

Al-Qaeda attacked Americans all 50 over the world.   It hoped that this would frighten Americans into leaving the Middle East.

Al-Qaeda hoped also that, by attacking America, it would 55 provoke the Americans to attack countries in the Middle East. This, it hoped, would make Muslims all over the world angry with America.   Then they would 60 join together and destroy America.

This is why, on 11 September, 2001, terrorists killed 3,000 people at the World Trade Center.

THINK ABOUT IT

Try to explain:

1. Why terrorists use terror.
2. What Osama bin Laden is trying to achieve.
3. Why at first he helped the Americans, but then attacked them.

STOP AND REFLECT: Al-Qaeda terrorists often die in their terrorist attacks, which are suicide missions. Think about this, on your own, in silence, for a while, and then finish this sentence:

'Al-Qaeda terrorists …'

In 1998, al-Qaeda blew up the American embassies in two African countries, killing 224 people.

SOURCE A

What does the September 11 attack tell us about a divided world?

On the morning of 11 September, 2001, 19 terrorists took over four jet planes.

5 The terrorists knew how to fly the planes. They flew two of them into the Twin Towers of the New York World Trade Center. The Twin Towers were part of America's trade with the rest of the world.
10 They were also important because they were the tallest buildings in New York.

The planes crashed into the Towers. Each plane carried 90,000
15 litres of petrol, which blew up, causing a huge fire. For those above the fires, there was no hope. Only four of them lived. 200 people jumped to their deaths
20 rather than burn in the fires. But the crashes and the fires had weakened the buildings. In the end, a whole floor fell down, crashing down on those
25 underneath, and the buildings collapsed. 2,800 people died. 1,500 people were crushed and burned to nothing.

A third plane crashed into the
30 Pentagon – the headquarters of the American army. About 200 people died, including the 64 people who were on the plane.

A fourth plane – Flight 93 – was heading for the White House, 35 where the President of America lives. This plane had 38 people on board. Some of them attacked the terrorists to stop them getting to the White House. The plane 40 crashed, killing them all.

THINK ABOUT IT

1. The targets on 11 September were not just important buildings, they were SYMBOLS. Explain why terrorists chose to attack:
   - The World Trade Center.
   - The Pentagon.
   - The White House.

2. Were the Americans to blame for the attacks in any way?

3. Bin Laden wanted:
   - To get al-Qaeda in the news.
   - To provoke America to attack Muslim countries.
   - To get support from other Muslims.

Did the attack of 11 September help his cause, do you think?

SOURCE Ⓐ

1. 8:45 am.
The first plane is flown into the north tower of the World Trade Center.

2. 9:03 am.
A second plane is flown into the south tower.

3. Both towers are on fire.
People start to leave.
Fireman go into the burning towers.

4. 10:00 am.
The south tower collapses.

5. 10:28 am.
The north tower collapses.

The Twin Towers of the World Trade Center.

Pulling it Together

Where do we go from here?

At the start of this book you were asked:

Can we look forward to the 21st century?

Look back and see what you said.

1. Look back through this book and find:

   - Two problems which the 20th century solved.

   - Two problems which we still have today.

2. Can terrorism be stopped?

3. Will the poor of the world ever get a fair share of the world's wealth?

4. Do you know of any other problems which the 21st century will have to cope with?

Stand up in front of the class and give a short talk, starting either:

- 'I am hopeful for the 21st century because …', or:

- 'I am fearful for the 21st century because …'

Try to make your talk as long as possible, and to make a number of points in support of your case.

GLOSSARY

Armistice the name for the official ceasefire at the end of the First World War

Blighty a First World War nickname for England

Bolsheviks the name for a fanatical Communist group in Russia

boycott when people refuse to go to something – for instance, the Nazi boycott of Jewish shops in Germany after 1933

censored where the government does not allow a certain piece of news or information to be published

Cold War the war between Russia and America, 1945–1989. Both sides had nuclear weapons and a 'hot war' would have meant that both sides were destroyed – so the two sides did everything they could to oppose each other except start fighting

Collectivisation Stalin's process of uniting small peasant farms into large whole-village ones

Communism / Communist a kind of government based on the ideas of Karl Marx where the government owns all the businesses, and shares the wealth equally between the people

Conscientious Objectors people who refuse to fight in a war

conscription where a government calls up men to fight in its army

deloused the process of killing lice which have attached themselves to the body, usually by covering the body in disinfectant powder

democracy government by the people, for the people – with elections where people vote their leaders into power

depression a period when prices fall and unemployment rises

dictator a ruler who has all-power in a country – a good example of a dictator was Adolf Hitler in Germany, 1933–1945

famine where harvests fail and people die of starvation

Fascism / Fascist a kind of government based on the idea that some races and some people are superior. The best example of a fascist government was the Nazi government of Germany, 1933–1945

Final Solution the Nazi plan to kill all the Jews in Europe, worked out at the Wannsee Conference in 1942

ghettos areas of a town where Jews were forced to go to live

Holocaust the Nazi attempt to gas and burn all the Jews in Europe, 1942–1945

Hoovervilles shanty towns of unemployed and poor people in America in the Depression of the late 1920s

hyper-inflation a time when prices rise out of control

independence where a country breaks away from an empire and gets its freedom

Iron Curtain Winston Churchill's name for the border between democratic western Europe and Communist eastern Europe during the Cold War

kulaks the rich peasants who did not like collectivisation – Stalin killed them

Luftwaffe the Nazi airforce

master-race the Nazi term to describe the 'Aryans' – the mythical super-race they thought superior to other races

no-man's-land the area – usually 100 m of mud and craters – between the two trench lines on a battlefield on the western front during the First World War

nuclear missiles long-range missiles with atomic warheads

pacifists people who oppose war

patriotism love of one's country

propaganda biased information published by a government to manipulate people to believe what it wants them to believe

racist a person who believes that some races are superior to others; usually it involves a hatred for 'lower' races. The worst example of racism was the Nazi treatment of the Jews, 1933–1945

revolution where a people rise up and attack their own government.

Soviets the name for Workers' Councils in communist Russia

SS the Nazi elite guard, who acted as Hitler's bodyguard and the concentration camp guards

suffragettes women who fought to get the vote

terrorism where a group secretly attacks the government by planting bombs, assassinations etc.

Tsar the name for the ruler of Russia until 1917

volunteer where men go to join up because they want to fight in the army

Index